PRAISE FOR

Under 35: The New Generation of American Poets

"There are poems in here that can save your life . . ."
—Gordon Lish

"Although many of these poets have been students, even my students, in the American workshop system, the poems that Nicholas Christopher has chosen by them and by the others have nothing to do with workshops, with juvenilia, or with pedagogy: they are poems of remarkable achievement, interest, and value, and I am delighted to read them together in this book." **—Richard Howard**

"In many of these poets, I find much of what will still be new when old, combined with what is most nearly absolutely new, now."
—A. R. Ammons

"Finally it doesn't matter to a generation of poets and their readers which individual poets write the great poems of that time; what matters, crucially, is that they be written. In this book Nicholas Christopher has collected evidence that the job is taken up and in good hands." **—William Matthews**

UNDER

35

the new generation

of American poets

AN ANCHOR BOOK

NEW YORK

LONDON

TORONTO

SYDNEY

AUCKLAND

EDITED BY

UNDER 35

the new generation
of American poets

NICHOLAS CHRISTOPHER

An Anchor Book

Published by Doubleday, a division of Bantam
Doubleday Dell Publishing Group, Inc., 666 Fifth
Avenue, New York, New York 10103

Anchor Books, **Doubleday**, and the portrayal of
an anchor are trademarks of Doubleday, a division
of Bantam Doubleday Dell Publishing Group, Inc.

Library of Congress Cataloging-in-Publication Data
[to come]

ISBN 0-385-26035-0

Acknowledgments for individual poems appear on pages [to come].

Copyright © 1989 by Nicholas Christopher

All Rights Reserved

Printed in the United States of America

Book design by Chip Kidd

April 1989

First Edition

CWO

Contents

The use of this symbol (■   ■   ■) at the bottom of the page indicates a stanza break.

UNDER 35

the new generation
of American poets

About the Editor

Nicholas Christopher was born in 1951, and graduated from Harvard College. He is the author of three books of poetry, *On Tour With Rita* (Knopf, 1982), *A Short History of the Island of Butterflies* (Viking, 1986), and *Desperate Characters: A Novella in Verse & Other Poems* (Viking, 1988) and a novel, *The Soloist* (Viking, 1986). The recipient of numerous awards, most recently Poetry Fellowships from the National Endowment for the Arts and the New York Foundation for the Arts and an Amy Lowell Traveling Fellowship, he is a frequent contributor to *The New Yorker* and has published his work widely in leading magazines and literary journals. He lives in New York City and teaches at New York University.

Introduction

The young American poet today is a poet of Empire. Empire in decline, from all indications. The contemporary reader of poetry in this country ought to feel right at home with the lyric poets of imperial Rome's rise and fall—Juvenal, Martial, Persius—in whose work we find, even more brilliantly refined and delineated, that same raw material that has so appealed to historians. Tales of corruption, greed, intrigue (high and low), militarism (complemented by military bungling and adventurism abroad), fantastic turns of fortune, public and private. Squalor and privation coexisting with astonishing opulence. Charlatans and confidence men abounding, from the pinnacles of government to the lowliest slums. Reckless ambition. Religious fanatics. Elaborate crimes. Social frivolity. Sensationalism. And violent games and spectacular pageantry to distract the masses of men when their noses are not to the wheel, keeping the Empire's machinery humming along, and to allay their collective fears and anxieties.

Such times are the best and worst for poets. They are never lacking for material: the high comedies of the powerful and the terrible tragedies of the weak, the sagas of love and sacrifice and redemption that seem to proliferate in turbulent eras, the labyrinthine scandals, and the roller-coaster mentality that a war economy (through wars "hot" and "cold") fosters, throw forth more subject matter than the poetic imagination can possibly deal with. Cosmopolitan poets and satirists have a field day. Pastoral poets, celebrants of natural beauty fleeing the metropolis (necessarily the heart of Empire), also tend to flourish, as do elegists, harking back to more golden days, and their religious and visionary brethren, making inner journeys in fluctuating states of rapture and alarm. For all of them, the downside is that their times are often not just hard, but spiritually barren, their readership dull, and their artistic validity—the number of citizens they actually reach with their work, however scintillating—often nil in the face of illiteracy, a mercantilist ethos, and in our own times, an enervating popular culture that is attuned to the lowest possible denominator of sensibility.

If this has the ring of a jeremiad, so be it. For every poet is writing not only his or her personal history, but also a history of his times. And an anthology such as this is, perforce, more a history of its times than a mere miscellany. The poets herein have come of age in a particularly charged and divided era. All were born at least nine years after Hiroshima, most during the Eisenhower presidency; at the height of the Vietnam War, few were over ten years old; in their earliest years, they lived through the assassination of one president, and eleven years later saw another resign in disgrace. They are full-fledged members of the television generation, and in their homes grew up watching, often in vivid color, wars, famines and aviation disasters, as well as incredible and heroic feats—men walking on the moon, flying across the seafloor, diverting rivers. Cultural and technological words and phrases unknown even to their older siblings at the same age—much less to their parents—were familiar to them in elementary school: "nuclear umbrella," "A-OK," "hot line," "silicon breasts," "heart transplant," "microchip," "macrobiotic," "acid trip," and so on. Like every generation, they are of course children of their times, and from a myriad of angles, their poetry reflects it, in strokes broad and exquisite, their voices caustic, gentle, incendiary, devotional.

That they are all Americans, dealing with an overwhelming subject by definition—gigantic, blunt, and intricate all at once—is evident, I believe, as soon as one begins turning the pages of this book. "The U.S.A. [is] a big operation, very big," Saul Bellow has written, "the more *it*, the less *we*." These poets, like all imperial poets worth their salt, are waging a constant war to reverse that ratio. And at its core this is not a political question, for the line of friction between that *it* and that *we* is fundamentally spiritual and artistic. It is drawn along the dark and luminous, ever-shifting ground from which our poets have taken their inspiration since the days of Anne Bradstreet and Philip Freneau. It is the tightrope the individual treads—or dances along—in a mass society. How these poets are dealing with their enormous subject, and working their way along this line, is what this book is about.

Their diversity, poetic and otherwise, is considerable. Among the contributors are Texans, Virginians, and Coloradans; big city poets from Chicago, New Orleans, and New York; town dwellers from Newburyport, Massachusetts, Los Osos, California, and Bloomington, Indiana. They make their livings as actors, lawyers, librarians, psychotherapists, filmmakers, and rock musicians. A number, as one might expect, work as editors and teachers. One woman is a former Pinkerton's security guard and one of the men once toiled as a professional knife thrower in a circus. Several are parents. A few are students, pursing advanced degrees. If one were so inclined, he could dig through their résumés for wonderful correspondences: a poet in Manhattan serving a residency in a cathedral; another who is studying biblical Greek in Assisi, Italy; and another who once labored as an "assistant bricklayer in a Ukranian monastery."

As an editor, I tried to leave behind all the axes I might have to grind—aesthetic, philosophical, and otherwise—when I began this venture. I tried to solicit and choose work to which I might not have been predisposed at another time, as a casual reader. My sole criterion, aside from the age and nationality requirements, was to ask myself whether a given poem jumped off the page for me, whether its language was charged, verbally and musically, so that the poet's world became our world. In making my selections, concerning myself with questions of craft and form, of variety and originality, I always tried to keep in mind Vladimir Nabokov's ideal: the poem that sends a tingle up the spine. All of these poems, at the very least, aspire to that ideal, and I leave it to the reader which of them may achieve it.

I used all the resources at my disposal to track down worthy and exciting potential contributors, and so if a particular favorite of the reader's has been omitted, it is due not to lack of diligence or open-mindedness, but to the sheer volume of very fine poetry being produced by young American poets, and to the amount of time, and space, available to me.

Behind all the clamor and clatter of daily life in America, and the terrifying distractions thereof, every poet must keep his finger on the one true pulse beat from which he draws his inspiration—the one which, however vibrantly or dimly, echoes the vast multitude of chambers in the human heart. The poet's business is to see "through," not "with," the eye, as William Blake advises, and to discern the fleeting configurations, phantoms, and illuminations that others might not see at all, or even dream of. And in freezing, and giving permanence, to what is ephemeral, and may be most significant, the inspired poet, especially in a time of Empire, is surely, in matters of the spirit, always providing us with freshly turned ground, leading us to our deepest selves, chronicling our dream life, and bit by bit constructing the truest history of his times, the one we shall return to, with pleasure and anticipation and a touch of sadness, to renew ourselves.

—Nicholas Christopher
New York City, January 1989

NOTE: Many friends and colleagues helped lead me to the work of poets I might not otherwise have come across, and I am most grateful to them. I would especially like to thank Anthony Hecht, Richard Howard, John Ashbery, David Lehman, J. D. McClatchy, Alice Quinn, Gordon Lish, Vickie Karp, and Cynthia Zarin for their generous assistance, and Heidi von Schreiner and the editorial staff at Anchor Books for their kind support.

JUDITH BAUMEL

The New York City World's Fairs, 1939 and 1964

for my mother

We visited the World's Fair
thirteen times and saved a brochure
from every pavilion.
When you were my age then,
with a Heinz pickle pin
on a brownie collar,
you trooped through the Dawn of a New Day,
the World of Tomorrow;
marched up the Helicline
and saw Billy Rose's Aquacade.
You went back for the thrill
of stepping on a board that yelled,
"ouch, that hurts" or "don't tread on me."
GM's bright Futurama between
the Great Depression
and the Second Great War.
I put 50 cents in a machine
at the Sinclair pavilion and it produced
a fresh warm plastic dinosaur.
That was man and science—
dinosaur to oil, oil to plastic.
I wanted and got another.
You wanted to teach the family possibilities,
to show man's clever exhibitions,
but the future I came away with
was an entire house
of impermeable Formica where I wept
because my brother was lost
for the fifth time that season
and you'd gone to some hamburger-
shaped tent to pick him up again.

Proper Distance and Proper Time

Two events have a spacelike separation.
Show that a frame can be found in which
the two events occur at the same time.

All summer he taught relativity
and knew their first time around
they wouldn't understand it
—that intuition of the weight of numbers.
Nothing visual helped:
Explosions on trains.
Twins separated and aging differently.
The pole vaulter running through a barn
so fast the pole shrinks by half
to the size of the barn.
He looked always to one student's squint
and tightened lip, for her form bent
over gas tubes in lab.

At the end they all drove out
to a field to watch the mid-August
meteor shower. He lay next to her
under a college blanket
separate but so close he imagined
the pressure of her knee
through blue jeans melting him.
Then they slept. Her knee as she curled
brushed him and he woke
absolutely still till she shifted away.
In the morning he told her
she was beautiful.
She considered Einstein's paradox:

■ ■ ■

If I hold a mirror in front of myself
arm's length away
and run at nearly the speed of light
will I be able to see myself?

Orcio and Fiasco

The flat underbellied fish-shaped scar on his forehead,
imprinted as if a fossil were imbedded and bleached
there, asked for explanation, to be read.

His text began with his car and the fish bucket he reached
out to to keep upright through a sharp curve
that sent him swerving over the road's edge into the breach

of terraced olive groves and vineyards that serve
in this utilitarian landscape for systems of heaven and hell,
the graded charts and maps that still preserve

the mnemonic fidelity of the Divine Comedy, as well
as the frescoes which derive from it, as living documentary.
And the Lord put a Fiat Cinquecento on those Tuscan hills

crashing with the logic of the Road Runner or Bugs Bunny.
A bucket, muddy water, worms, all the tackle, all the fish
flying separately through the car as the car flew. An elementary

physics film illustrating the first moment of undiminished
movement, lines and arrows, trajectory of water, momentum,
acceleration, vectors, gravity the same as in the Pisan parish.

Or it might be fear animate in a many-panelled pastel cartoon
of objects tumbling in energetic spirals skewed
into a chaos of crosses, stars and expletives, suns and moons.

■ ■ ■

Either way—approximate emotive sketches that won't hurt you
or compass-precise diagrams—neither one is the truth and both
just describe a human order we insinuate upon divine virtue.

JUDITH BAUMEL

Fish Speaking Veneto Dialect

G
as
tro
nom
ists
remark
that the
fish of
the Adri-
atic is   a-
mongst the best
in the world. And
what does the fish
have to say about
this? Nothing, other-
wise what kind of fish
is he? As mute as a fish,
as the Italian saying goes.
We should learn our lesson
from this and perhaps not
keep silent but chatter a
bit less. In the beginning . . .
there was the fish when, just
after the year 1000, the Veneto
people of the mainland sought
refuge on a small group of islands scattered just above the
surface of the water around a
deep canal, the rivus prealtus.
Fish, lots and lots of fish,
in Venice and Chioggia, on
Murano and Burano, where
the humblest fishermen are
just like the makers of the
most intricate, delicate
lace. The fish is a real
democrat, his metamorpho-
sis rather adaption to
the environment and to
the situation. Poor
with the poor and
rich with the rich.
In the past cer-
tainly, but today
. . . it depends,
all the world is
changing. A
history of
people seen
through
fish has
not been
written
yet. But it must
include Doge Andrea
Gritti (whose massive bulk
was painted several times by Titian)
who died on 28 December 1538 at the
venerable old age of 83, having just eaten an
enormous meal of eel on the spit. Pace all'anima sua.

BRUCE BEASLEY

Sleeping in Santo Spirito

Shut out
of Masaccio's chapel where I'd tried
three times to see Eve and Adam

hunted by the angel, hiding
their genitals and eyes,
this afternoon I went instead

to sleep in the damp heat
of Santo Spirito. I watched
a priest in a black cassock,

swinging his silver censer, mount
the high altar to the Host
suspended among gold

to remake it into flesh.
Filthy, half-asleep, I thought
how the Gnostics wore black

to grieve
the soul's imprisonment in the flesh,
the light

buried inextricably in the dark body.
I watched him
consecrate and crack

■ ■ ■

the brittle tablet, dissolving it
bit by bit on his tongue,
mumbling

Corpo di Cristo . . . Hunched
low in my seat at the dim
back of the altar, I fell

asleep as the congregation
rose in communion, their hymn
resounding foreign

and hollow across the vaulted glass.
My body was fouled
with sweat: I'd walked

miles to see the *Expulsion*, and stood
spent before the scaffolded chapel,
its door

draped with a cartoon of the two
tormented figures. Aching
all over, I saw

that shut chapel again as I breathed
the holy smoke
of Santo Spirito, the votive

candles still burning
behind my eyes. The black
back-wings of the stone angel

■ ■ ■

smeared into sleep, with the wooden
donation boxes for the souls
of Purgatory, only

the faraway wailing of the mass
holding me up.
I woke to a black-cloaked monk

staring me down, his harsh
eyes accusing me of sickness
or sacrilege; slouched

over a dark pew
carved with gnarled
gargoyles, I was caught

half-asleep in the house of the holy ghost.

Childhood

In Macon, the paper mill
used to fill the night air
with a stench before rain—
acrid, decayed,
                    like burnt garbage . . .

I didn't understand why rain
required such a warning, a burning-off.

On the back porch in summer, the air
felt tense, expectant—
a siren sounding closer & closer to home,

two flies caught, & furious, in the torn screen,

the dark, sharp-tipped
leaves pointing over the stormclouds . . .

Then a clearing: smell of street dust,
& each star exactly in its place around the pecan tree,

all hesitant & dim, anchoring, waiting their time.

The Reliquary

I wait gluttonously for God
                —Rimbaud

All over Italy, the saints'
bodies are scattered,
brittle, barely
durable, St. Jerome's
one finger pointing the way.

There's a black
nail from Calvary, the sallow
bone of a wrist, splinters
from the cross, and under
stained glass, the dark
figurines: Christ
on the cross, a wooden
Joseph and Mary
kneeling in their creche.

How simple
they seem, like a child's
sad prayer before sleep, or the sure
words of a catechism
we barely recall.

And the canvases,
so casually
crowded with angels
and saints who bear,
too soon, their martyrdom:

■ ■ ■

Sebastian,
already burdened with arrows,
attends the Virgin and Child,
and Mary
submits to the stern
angel, already
admitting the strange
embryo into her womb.

Over an altar, Titian's
Virgin is flown
into heaven, her red
robes trailing through the dim
church, the painting
left like a vestige of her body
that has so long been
withdrawn, abruptly
assumed . . .

If the body
is a temple of the Holy Ghost,
the saints'
bodies, scattered piece by piece
from Palermo to Ravenna,
are fallen

temples, like Michelangelo's
smashed Pietà,
locked like a relic behind glass
in St. Peter's,

healed and still.

■ ■ ■

When we left
Santa Maria Novella, the sky
was dark and the pigeons
swarmed,
pecking for bread;

the square was empty and the moon
rose close to the church, the heavens
glossed over, opening and closing
through the clouds, with an eerie

backlight like the thick
glass of a reliquary, enclosing
the rich and secret odor of decay.

APRIL BERNARD

The Way We Live Now

Sed quid agas? Sic vivitur.
                    —*Cicero*

COME AS YOU ARE
The difficulties, in passion,
are not news: the knot at the throat,
the lipstick that smears, the skirt
which induced such provocative hobbling
yet will not rise above the thighs.
So many comedies of the zipper,
the shoelace, and the coiffure.
Similarly, the aria will not soar
if the diva is sitting down.
We do not advocate nudity, exactly, nor
the slattern in the unbelted kimono
swigging beer from a bottle by the electric fan.
Yet how are we to stand and sing
in purple raincoats, gather rosebuds
from a moving train?
It was during the salad course,
and the fifth bottle of wine,
when a shot was fired, and the power failed,
that we realized we had not dressed for this.

THE AERIALISTS
Vain, cantankerous, gentle,
undaunted by truths,
unconquerable as the dirt,
with such a smile. . . .

■ ■ ■

18

Escaped balloons graze
the rotunda dome while the reception
pastures beneath: let us float like that,
let us rise above

If I could get to the truth,
it would not be your Melvyn Douglas satin robe,
the fits of withdrawal, the late-blooming evenings,
the evil clouds of smoke, eyes that smile and sorrow
and are not fooled, as by Memling. . . .

SATAN MOVES MYSTERIOUSLY

We seek a slogan, and find only the old ones.
We need revolution, but settle
for bad manners. Who will be the one
to strip the uniform of its stars,
splash mud on the trousers of El Exigente,
while the state's borders are ringed
by lethal picket fence posts?
A few men have been towering over us,
blocking the light in the city streets.
Meanwhile, hands are blown off, crops die,
buildings implode; perishing, want, and sorrow follow.
Not enough left in my mouth to spit.

ALTERNATE ROUTE

Have pity, oh have pity
for the clenched hand that beats upon the breast,
declaring, I have done this,
I have not done that, it's all been
all my fault.
But not for the woman in the red wrap dress
and pink carnation corsage
singing "Quando, Quando, Quando."
Not guilt, but accusation;
neither tears, nor mild laughter—
This is where I have found you, after all,
walking down Sixth Street on a hot day in May:

green sunglasses, black leather—
exact in period costume;
comical in passion,
redeemed, redeemed, redeemed;
ready to give up the ghosts,
to give everything away.

Elephant Languor

Some days go by "like elevators," while others do not.
On the elephant day, whimsy creeps up like the bad old friend at a party,
to dish, or nuzzle, or tweak off your lint,
and you may compromise with a smile.
In the closeness, especially then, do the tricks come calling:
the fat sleepy mother of three who rolls in the tide pool,
the gull eviscerating whelks on the tar road,
the collapse of the scrub forest on your near right,
that which avails through cloud cover and brands your knee.
Impatient with length, so as to approximate the fast (unfastness)
of our days, reluctant to suspend for as long as it takes—
Except on the elephant day, swaggering with its here-to-there on bolster pins
to the tune of Baby Walk When His Red Ones In The Wash,
and Garter Snake Lie Like A Noodle On The Rock. . . .
And all of it, all of it, too long to be endured
except for the slow mercy of self-pity, a smiling *tendence*
to unroll the carpet wherein our wicked treasures hide,
and spread it out and take the elephants walking and crunching,
one by one, so that in these pulverizing steps thyme, and mint, and pennyroyal
rise up in their sweetness and dawdle the days past clocking

Ten Years Apprenticeship in Fantasy*

My Darling C,

There is something to be said for Nature after all, dusk pending, variable stars. I have had a change in luminosity.

All winter long, I've tried not to write to you. There is something too final to it I should think. First, news of America: the farmers are being winnowed out again. Now that I have cable television, I am in touch with the world. In the rain last night, rice went for twenty-five cents a pound in the midwest. Blacks lined the barnlike edges of their city, umbrellaed by eaves & politics & the fair price of near-proteins. I, myself, as you know, have been starving alternately for a decade. Everyone wants to know why & I tell them it's my way of holding the world back.

Also, on the evening news, I saw a six-legged steer. The father (his master) reports that Beauty is in the Eye of the Beholder. He loves that thing. Everyone wants to know how many hearts it has. Only one.

In the more immediate vicinity of my house where—you should know, it is just on the verge of twilight—I have courted this darkness lying face down into my hands all afternoon, absolutely loathing the light, doing Gestalt fantasies (you're allowed, I hear, to feel healthy in erotic dreams of submission), waiting for an orange moon to bloom into the nightsky, waiting for absolute quiet, waiting to get vulnerable again.

■ ■ ■

Where I used to live, the fog slid off the great bourbon-colored mountain to roost around my house at dawn. It was as thick as a religious cough. Here, cats come down the corridors of the city streets like the selected survived. No one is rich anymore. The extended family makes its comeback in the clapboard houses where all porch-sitting has been suspended until spring.

There's a big to-do about lymphocytes & immunities, what with all of us living so close together, the quick, violent, unapproachable deaths of so many of us here. The body's weather allows each germ to enter musically: ethereal, fullblown. Of lymphocytes, I imagine they are one-celled stars in the big liquid chambers of the body underwater: glowing & attentive, lighting the way as they linger in that great invertebrate chain of hankering.

I know you get depressed when I get all lofty like this. I've been reading the Romantics since two o'clock. Even the poets married. I find comfort in this fact, though it besieges me with awe. Those of us who are susceptible to weather might be marred by the great heaving effort of the winter as it turns.

As I approach evening I wait for the sound of stars crackling. I have never heard this noise, not yet. I imagine it is never cool there in the long, bright, monolithic hour of each star. It tickles me, actually, that this light received expired long before I ever spoke. Like this letter, which, if passed from hand to hand, will reach you long after I am gone. This moment will continue for as long as you imagine/ *Me. Until the star goes blank & quivers/ Until it becomes vividly cold/ Possessed by an old/ Gravity & falls.*

In closing, let me remind you of the Siamese twins separated not long ago in Canada. They let the little one, the concave half, be girl. Without her, he will skip quicker, eat more heartily, raise up his own kind & I think he should be given that one good chance. What better reason to go on living than to repeat yourself autobiographically? She didn't have that chance you understand.

■ ■ ■

I know the storm has reached past your knees by now & the electricity falters & the mail has become erratic & you're living on your thoughtful supply of canned goods. Don't let your teeth & hair get weak, as certain vitamins & minerals are missed sorely in a bland diet of single-minded sustenance. Pray only that the heat inside lasts until this thing has passed. Stay up all night if you have to, to avoid bad dreaming. It can hurt you & I need you. I am, as ever, yours.

*The title for "Ten Years Apprenticeship in Fantasy" refers to John Keats's request to be given a decade in which to indulge himself, watching the world before writing it all down. The epigraph for the poem, taken from "Sleep and Poetry" is as follows: "O for ten years, that I may overwhelm/ Myself in Poesy; so I may do the deed/ That my own soul has to itself decreed."

After the Grand Perhaps*

After vespers, after the first snow
has fallen to its squalls, after New Wave,
after the anorexics have curled
into their geometric forms,
after the man with the apparition
in his one bad eye has done red things
behind the curtain of the lid & sleeps,
after the fallout shelter in the elementary school
has been packed with tins & other tangibles,
after the barn boys have woken, startled
by foxes & fire, warm in their hay, every part
of them blithe & smooth & touchable,
after the little vandals have tilted
toward the impossible seduction
to smash glass in the dark, getting away
with the most lethal pieces, leaving
the shards which travel most easily
through flesh as message
on the bathroom floor, the parking lots,
the irresistible debris of the neighbor's yard
where he's been constructing all winter long.
After the pain has become an old known
friend, repeating itself, you can hold on to it.
The power of fright, I think, is as much
as magnetic heat or gravity.
After what is boundless: wind chimes,
fertile patches of the land,
the ochre symmetry of fields in fall,
the end of breath, the beginning
of shadow, the shadow of heat as it moves
the way the night heads west,
I take this road to arrive at its end
where the toll taker passes the night, reading.
I feel the cupped heat

of his left hand as he inherits
change; on the road that is not his road
anymore I belong to whatever it is
which will happen to me.

    When I left this city I gave back
the metallic waking in the night, the signals
of barges moving coal up a slow river north,
the movement of trains, each whistle
like a woodwind song of another age
passing, each ambulance would split a night
in two, lying in bed as a little girl,
a fear of being taken with the sirens
as they lit the neighborhood in neon, quick
as the fire as it takes fire
& our house goes up in night.

    After what is arbitrary: the hand grazing
something too sharp or fine, the word spoken
out of sleep, the buckling of the knees to cold,
the melting of the parts to want,
the design of the moon to cast
unfriendly light, the dazed shadow
of the self as it follows the self,
the toll taker's sorrow
that we couldn't have been more intimate.

    Which leads me back to the land,
the old wolves which used to roam on it,
the one light left on the small far hill
where someone must be living still.

    After life there must be life.

*After the Grand Perhaps was inspired by these alleged final words of Francois Rabelais: "I am going to seek a grand perhaps; draw the curtain, the farce is played."

Domestic Mysticism*

In thrice 10,000 seasons, I will come back to this world
In a white cotton dress. Kingdom of After My Own Heart.
Kingdom of Fragile. Kingdom of Dwarves. When I come home,
Teacups will quiver in their Dresden saucers, pentatonic chimes
Will move in wind. A covey of alley cats will swarm on the side
Porch & perch there, portents with quickened heartbeats
You will feel against your ankles as you pass through.

After the first millenium, we were supposed to die out.
You had your face pressed up against the coarse dyed velvet
Of the curtain, always looking out for your own transmigration:
What colors you would wear, what kind of jewel,
What kind of pageantry, if your legs would be tied
Down, if Down, if there would be wandering tribes of minstrels
Following with woodwinds in your wake.

This work of mine, the kind of work which takes no arms to do,
Is least noble of all. It's peopled by Wizards, the Forlorn,
The Awkward, the Blinkers, the Spoon-Fingered, Agnostic Lispers,
Stutterers of Prayer, the Closet Weepers, the Flatulent,
The Charlatans. I am one of those. In January, the month the owls
Nest in, I am a witness & a small thing altogether. The Kingdom
Of Ingratitude. Kingdom of Lies. Kingdom of *How Dare I*.

I go on dropping words like little pink fish eggs, unawares, slightly
Illiterate, often on the mark. Waiting for the clear whoosh
Of fluid to descend & cover them. A train like a silver
Russian love pill for the sick at heart passes by
My bedroom window in the night at the speed of mirage.
In the next millennium, I will be middle aged. I do not do well
In the marrow of things. Kingdom of Trick. Kingdom of Drug.

■ ■ ■

In a lung-shaped suburb of Virginia, my sister will be childless
Inside the ice storm, forcing the narcissus. We will send
Each other valentines. The radio blowing out
Vaughan Williams on the highway's purple moor.
At nine o'clock, we will put away our sewing to speak
Of lofty things while, in the pantry, little plants will nudge
Their frail tips toward the light we made last century.

When I come home, the dwarves will be long
In their shadows & promiscuous. The alley cats will sneak
Inside, curl about the legs of furniture, close the skins
Inside their eyelids, sleep. Orchids will be intercrossed & sturdy.
The sun will go down as I sit, thin armed, small breasted
In my cotton dress, poked with eyelet stitches, a little lace,
In the queer light left when a room snuffs out.

I draw a bath, enter the water as a god enters water:
Fertile, knowing, kind, surrounded by glass objects
Which could break easily if mishandled or ill-touched.
Everyone knows an unworshipped woman will betray you.
There is always that promise, I like that. Kingdom of Kinesis.
Kingdom of Benevolent. I will betray as a god betrays,
With tenderheartedness. I've got this mystic streak in me.

*According to Herodotus, the ancient Egyptians believed that, after death, the human soul had to pass through various forms of incarnation for a period of 3,000 years. Plato, in *The Phaedrus*, set the period at 10,000 years (which the Philosophic Soul could reduce to a mere 3,000-year period). In *The Republic*, however, he calculates that the departed souls had to spend 1,000 years before returning to this world. In "Domestic Mysticism," the formula of exile is derived from Empedocles, who reckoned the period of the soul's transmigration as "thrice ten-thousand seasons," or 2,500 years.

CYRUS CASSELLS

La Luna Verde

for Lorca

> *Green, how I love you, green.*
> *Green wind. Green branches.*
> *Ship on the sea,*
> *galloping horse on the mountain.*
> *With the shadow on her waist,*
> *she dreams by her railing,*
> *green hair, green flesh . . .*
> *—Lorca, "Sleepwalking Ballad"*

Suddenly the cante jondo chord of a guitar,
like wine spilling onto white cloth,
and your words, after so many years,
"Verde que te quiero verde,"
green, how I love you, green,
as in an open-air café, I feel myself
a student again, a young translator,
carrying my frayed copy
of *Romancero Gitano*, taking up the old quarrel
whether the moon is blue
or green.
Federico, at seventeen, I became possessed
by your voice in Andalucía, in Nueva York.
I loved you then
—as the chronicler of the gypsies,
as the visionary traveler
who mourned for Harlem.
You were my poet of blood and quicksilver,
of nard and moonlight—a sentient arrow
piercing me, as I tried to capture

the duende of your "Romance Sonámbulo"
—in the act of translation,
trying to make the leap
into your life,
which I make now, simply,
as the guitar exudes
a slow bloom of wine,
and I begin
to imagine your death:
I close my eyes and see
a tiny plaza, a summer moon poised
above a fountain,
and near that fountain,
a man who must be you,
rapt, focusing
on the splash of the water,
so as not to hear
the sound of shots from the hills
outside Víznar
—Víznar, which has become
another Calvary.
You hear a ticking
and look up:
A small boy is tracing circles
around you, dragging a gnarled stick
over the stones.
You take out your last cigarette,
watching him, and lift it
almost to your lips—then freeze
as he stops, drops the stick,
and takes from his pocket
a blood orange.
He opens his fruit
and sucks;
shyly, remembering his manners,
he extends his juice-stained hand
and offers you pungence.
And then he sees Death in your gaze
and runs down a narrow street.

A man in uniform appears
and touches your shoulder, and says,
"Señor, wake up.
It's time for your paseo."
And you go quietly.

Now the plaza is empty;
there is nothing but the moonlight
on the stones, the slow splash
of the fountain.

At wolf's hour, at the dark base
of a sierra,
the night is so beautiful: a few stars
over the vega,
cicadas, in the cistern
a water of tambourines.
I watch a man blindfold you
and think of de Icaza's words:
". . . nothing in life can equal
the agony of being blind
in Granada."
A chord resonates.
A breeze of Moorish ghosts
stirs the olive grove,
and I whisper in your terrified ear:
"Verde viento. Verdes ramas."
Green wind. Green branches.
Federico, I want to be your eyes,
I want to touch you
the way your voice touched mine
when I was younger,
the way a woman stands on a balcony
during the saeta, gripping the iron railing
in both hands, and sings
to the image of the crucified Christ.

■ ■ ■

At dawn there is no sun,
only the green moon—lucent and everlasting.
In its light,
I can see them clearly, the patent-leather men
who have no use for poetry.
They'd turn the vega
into a killing floor.
But as they pull the triggers,
they breathe the landscape
which *is* your poem:

Federico, I saw—
the flesh on their hands was green.

Bound Feet

for Winston Tong

There was a woman of Ming snow.
In the name of love,
her feet were bound—so that a man might touch
the tiny shoes, and whisper
Lotus, lotus. . . . Her pained face flickered
on the surface of tea.
Behind her phoenix screen, the secret
cached in white cloth:
blood, crushed bone.

At festivals the women gathered, hobbling together,
a forest of canes—their bodies
the attitudes of willows—

For a thousand years, the women
were crippled into deer. In the name of love,
their souls froze into jade.

The Pillow

He touches her breasts, a sunburned neck, a back bent
from years in the fields.
And now she lifts to him in the moonlight
her belly, as pale
as a Nō mask—

It has been like this
for decades, the two of them
lying together on the futon:
See, their bodies have twisted
into an old branch.

Typhoon

In shade, on cardboard squares, the sleeping obaasan,
wizened women in white kerchiefs resting
from their work, their tray left
in the hall before me, bowls cleaned
of green tea and rice,
while carp gleam in the pond,
like agile gold, like lamps—suspended
as if in the body of their dream.

I slide back the shoji panel
to see more clearly, lift
American eyes—a stranger measuring
a haiku of calm.

But already in the distance
the clouds appear,
like a flaw in a delicate
landscape screen.

It is the season of typhoon:
Above green terraces of rice, the sky
lowers—

And the wind lifts off
the roof of sleep.

>   —Taki Ashina Yokosuka,
>   August 1978

V-Winged and Hoary

All our pink and gold and blue
birds have gone to Panama or Peru:

the willow flycatcher with its sneezy "fitzbew,"
the ruby-throated hummingbird with jewel-

like gorgets and the blue-rumped finch,
its song a warble with a guttural "chink."

Far, far across the ghostly frozen lake,
above the great drifts of snow swaying

like dunes, the frosty Iceland gulls,
pallid as beach fleas, make great loops and catfall

into the wind. They are all that is left.
Throngs of children tiptoe deftly

across the lake to watch the robust birds
plunge headlong into kamikaze dives, lured

by fledgling trout nosed against the shallow ice.
Despite the precarious ice,

the children huddle bundled at the edge:
mittened, scarved and starry-eyed,

■ ■ ■

their teeth chattering in the frosty air.
They watch the tireless birds, over and over,

fall from the speckled sky, their downy underwings
and pink, taloned leggings

foam-soaked as they grapple with their catch.
The children are in love with the miraculous

oval-lipped trout swimming upwards for air.
Snowflakes fall against their

cracked lips as they wait, their mouths agape
in little O's at the spectacle of gulls.

Desert Days on the Reservoir

Talking town but always
    thinking Christ! Christ!
Silly me, a hick
    in an evening jacket,

guest at a neighbor's
    pint-sized, terrace-lipped
house, a Trinity
    home of feathered brick—

Trinity, minus the Father
    and Spirit, ALL of us
sons (and sonless!)
    watching the sun go down

like a baby's head
    upon a vista of summer
and a jetsam of sultry air.
    Watch the rising stars,

brightest Vega on the zenith,
    a mica point
on a noiseless reservoir,
    where a terrapin glides

bankward, a speck of green,
    its flesh cozy
inside a diamondback,
    its horny beak wet-fresh

■ ■ ■

from a lunch of liquid grass.
    Now the speedboats,
breathless from their day
    of bouncing across the lake,

are snug in their slips,
    their engines propped
across their bows
    like the heads of sunbathers,

and the turtle makes its way,
    even now delirious
from the trough and chop
    of their wake.

From scent to scent:
    fumes from my tumbler of sweet
wine, the gillyflowers' aroma
    of clove beyond the terrace,

the squeak of sexuality,
    that ancient power
breaching our enclave of toms
    with its pirate of thirst.

Beneath a sky of aquatint,
    I do not know
my destination and watch
    the smoke pour from my

neighbor's lips like a sonnet
    of foam written
against the evening's
    late glimmer of sunlight.

■ ■ ■

Like animals at the zoo,
   we lounge and loll
in a world of seeming
    purity that leaves us dreaming,

all of us neat, prosaic
   figures reposed against these
desert days on the reservoir;
   all of us on the edge

of madness and effervescence,
   imagining ourselves
very near to heaven,
   despite the catalog of sins

behind us, and the peacock's
   imperious voice in each of us,
tiny as a sparrow, calling:
   "Catch the rising stars!"

Pure Valentine

In the orchestra it matters. Beards
become concerns as if it were a circus with dollars to be made
where everyone wakes up at sunrise,
gets cold with barn water, so their singing voices drop down
for a song sung importantly
to a low flower.

This is never done in a hamlet where
mothers come home on stretchers after a nightshift on the switchboard.
Awake, all voices sound big,
the diapason clear as in the best city's best auditorium
where all audiences are royal
or feel so feeling muted velvet on their cold necks.

Next to a closet kneels a boy
wanting to be inside, light a candle to undress Barbie dolls by,
and to read how Xygon, the Ibu prince, got his power, and
can he have some? His
brains creak now, take him to a cold tower,
acquit him from piano lessons,
nimble fingers better used on snaps
and strings, plastic pumps and tiny teacups.

Later, he is protected by geese on the soft edge of a windy lake.
It matters here that there be wind to cool his hot hair,
to teach him to use it for trumpet time, to slurp up air
like good dope smoke savored, then release something better,
bluer.

■ ■ ■

The truth is only practiced, not perfected to flaw
until you wear off-white and love a man named Devotion,
build a cool kitchen with free cats circumventing
like a seam on a purple yellow sari you watched spinning
as it stood on a bus.

In Rome how lost you'd be in antiquity with new people
reading newspapers upside down
and no genetics to weave a blonde for you to wink at.

It would have to be a boat
to justify your coming back here.

Xylophone Luncheonette

We began to dance
and soon
what got you strong
is what I loved

We'll own this place
and paint a sign for I-90:
Free Coffee and Donut
To Honeymooners

We stand
in party corners
drinkin' white lightning

We want to own a luncheonette
crimp pickles
shake chips
melt cheese on white toast
ice parsley &
music a mood
frantic as barn love

You're my lucky penny
got me off the highway crew
shorn my wig

Took me uptown
watched my shimmy said

Now

That's all right

Silver Nakedness in Calumet City

Stark
to eyes sophistically shaded at night
the Candy Shack sign pokes pink light
Big   Money   Girls   Instant   Interview
So the powerful peppers on a drunk's tongue
keep him mumbling, like he's eating his lips
I love his confusion
and am proud of it like a darkened
prima donna   the way he bumps off cars
like a sea goat
Here, I have purple bottle finger
and a better echo   What's left
to do as lightning wets our arms outside
Johnnie's Snack Shop?   A girl passes with
"I'm wearing black because my vacation is dead."
And she's in it,
in on the hint Hammond train whistles give
that excitement is occurring
but elsewhere   they make me belly-up
and buy that hat   otherwise, it's
happenstance tacos from a tavern and
I can't make it in the country
shovels lasting like wedding cake unused
Virginia Plaines protects my robust women
with pool sticks
See their shadows and you've seen dedication
I find it everywhere   the thundering
dough balls of bygone days
This dead city agrees with the deader sea
it used to be   and it's tomahawking through me
tonight   until I crave a chili dog from a wagon
that drips through my hand   I hear,
"Isn't she a bit of a narrow saint?"   and Lizabeth

Scott crooning through her bangs somewhere up high
and this is my signal when the fan turns
Giuseppe Verdi means Joe Green
I try to see
what makes me sleep
the Indian woman in her sari
swinging on a swing

Ted Berrigan

Pit of Nanotchka
pray for me
chlorine my hair for me

Phoney Baloney San Antoni
isolate me
like a powder blue figure of Christ
on the ledge beside salt

Rubber Gloves
lurch at me
put a fire drill in my blood

run me up the stairs of the
Statue of Liberty
torture me this way then

banana breakfasts
banana lunches
banana torture me too

Cabin of Louie the Hermit
flirt with me
run the gamut from

sniffing the Band-Aid box
to an aspirin in my Coke

■ ■ ■

Ouija Board and Planchette
    guide me
        teach me to say yes and no

     closet me with
        an orthopedic saddle shoe
            on a tropical couch

All my secret friends
     rise like Baron von Richthofen
       keep me company
            and bring wine while you're at it

Are We Ready for the Jimi Hendrix Story?

for Laura Zasada

The movies wouldn't buy it
but the hospital story . . .
you walking home with
the rock from your knee bouncing in
formaldehyde with fluorescent POISON
stamped on it
clutched in front of you
like a beacon
getting followed by the baseball cap boys
who wanted you to have sex
with them
for money
or where can they find a girl
following you home and the big
tension
headache
How could they continue?
You showed them the poison
like a fish in your hands
didn't they know anything?

The Good Hands People Know Their Bodies

Solo violinists say how natural it is to play
with the chin rested and both arms above
the diaphragm level. They bellow their backs
in order to breathe, extending and arcing
in a manner fitting a concertina.
It is when inexperienced lungs wait
for breaks in fingering or sudden downbeat
strokes that their toes go into spasm,
the feet wanting to leave the floor.

French bakers say always check for bunions
before ordering fine breads and pastries.
The time it takes to learn rolling,
be able to change a dust bowl of clouds
into a sky of croissants, is exactly one bunion.
And the madness that follows, the rolling
well into the middle of the night
and the compensating, the eating of what doesn't rise
like indiscriminate ladyfingers, is the second.

Prostitutes say that underneath all the panting
and promising, they are not even near there at all.
Really they are remembering a sister's birthday
or making a grocery list of orange juice and jelly.
Letting the body feel something is the lowest form
of infidelity, like a shrink jacking off behind the desk.
It's not part of the money. It's not part of the habit.
Sometimes, depending upon the person and the price,
it's not even faithful to think.

■ ■ ■

Some people believe in the power of Jesus,
say they have the ability to straighten backs
with the touch of their hands. Years of pain and anguish
vanish completely in a matter of seconds. But most clergy
confess simply that the way to be saved is not easy.
It must be done bit by bit, deed by deed, over and over.
God pays off for the labors of love. The bigger
the virtue the higher the premium. But the effort
is yours. You will soon be what you are now becoming.

Coroners report that no body is unremarkable.
Sometimes in suicides, they'll find advanced syphilis,
impending appendicitis, or right-sided hearts.
Even in plane crashes it is possible to tell
where most arms and legs go, their patterns leaving
a permanent impression. Some bodies, drifters,
refuse recognition, must be kept their entire shelf life,
until their bones settle down, assume a posture
long enough to be noticed.

My Mother in Majorca

My mother in Majorca for the summer writes a letter.

> *In Majorca, it's sun, hot and dry, cracking sun.*
> *In Majorca, it's rock, jagged and orcharded, olive rock.*
> *In Majorca, it's sea, mirroring and clear, isolating sea.*
> *Take it from me, I'm having a great time.*

My mother in Majorca searches for bodies.
A mountain fell there Before Christ, a landslide.
My mother in Majorca searches for survivors.

> *In Majorca, the expedition found a necklace.*
> *In Majorca, we dig and sift, shovel and scrape.*
> *Take it from me, there are four layers left to go.*

My mother in Majorca glues and pieces a people together.

> *In Majorca, we found an oven and some shards.*
> *In Majorca, the women bear, cook and clean, and bear, then die.*
> *Take it from me, your father expects a tight house.*
> *Take it from me, change the sheets on Mondays.*

My mother in Majorca imagines life.

> *In Majorca, they bury their dead with lime.*
> *In Majorca, people eat seafood and fruit, seafood and snails and olives.*
> *In Majorca, people drink.*
> *Take it from me, your brother needs food to grow.*
> *Take it from me, your father is nasty after a beer.*

My mother in Majorca catalogues.

In Majorca, Robert Graves walks into Deya to get his mail.
In Majorca, we sit in cafes late and talk, sit and talk.
Take it from me, your father comes home at eight.
Take it from me, your father needs attention.

My mother in Majorca compares two cultures.

In Majorca, people make coffee without filters.
In Majorca, children grow up in spite of parents.
Take it from me, these people never heard of Adler.

My mother in Majorca searches for survivors.
A depression ruptured the family in Houston, a rift.
My mother in Majorca writes home.

In Majorca, a Hilton is in Palma, a Hilton and other resorts.
In Majorca, they sell jewelry and coral, jewelry and olive-wood bowls.
In Majorca, the international papers are flown in daily.
Take it from me, I'm having a great time.

My mother in Majorca brings home her island.

Earth

Evelyn's lips are on the man next door.
She had been minding her own business weeding,
and was contemplating quitting,
it being so unbearably hot outside,
and worse, her neighbors at it again,
the husband finally painting the house
but brilliant green, and the wife red,
screaming the civic club will condemn them,
cars are already stopping to stare,
and he can go to hell for all she cares,
the sun all this while searing down,
and the husband asking and asking
for another beer, but the wife refusing,
finally calling him a drunken lout,
and him getting down off the ladder
and going to hit her, and her
picking up the can of paint
in retaliation and saying, Go ahead,
make my day. Then they relived
the fight from the day before,
he calling her a nag, she,
him a bad father, he,
her a bitch, she,
him a . . . a man,
and then it happened:
he grabbed his chest and fell down,
and she called, Come off it man,
do you expect me to believe that,
and then, Evelyn, Evelyn, come quick.

■ ■ ■

Evelyn is pumping now on Don's chest,
but he is not responding,
and when Susie comes back
from calling the ambulance,
Evelyn tells her to run across the street
and get Andy, her arms are getting tired,
and Andy, much bigger, would be better,
but everything will be all right,
she's had CPR. Andy, a cop,
also knows what to do and takes over
pumping on the count of three,
freeing Evelyn to do nothing but breathe,
but Don is still not responding,
and Andy starts screaming at him,
Come on, come on, come on.
He tells Evelyn to slap him
in the face while she's not breathing,
and to call his name. Evelyn pats him
on the cheek and says, Don, Don,
breathe, breathe. And Andy screams at her,
Louder, harder, and Evelyn slaps him in the face
and shouts, Don, Don, come on, come on.
But Andy shouts at her, Breathe, breathe,
and then, Louder still and harder,
and Evelyn boxes Don in the ear
and yells, Don you damn bastard,
nobody dies on me, nobody.

Indeed Don opens his eyes and looks
at her the look just before a scream,
but then exhales a complex syllable,
and they close, his body going suddenly
limp again, and Susie losing it,
crying, For crying out loud,
and, What Don what, and then running
down the street toward the ambulance.
The paramedics administer electroshock,
but nothing happens. They shock again,

and still nothing. And again and again,
giving him injections between each time,
and again and again and again,
and Evelyn screams at them to come on,
Nobody dies from heart attacks anymore,
call in the helicopter or something.
But they shake their heads
as if they're sorry lady,
and they load him into the ambulance,
shaking their heads again,
this time at Susie, he probably
doesn't have a chance.
Then a kid from the crowd comes up
to Evelyn and asks did she know
what happened, and Evelyn rubs
her hand over her mouth,
the taste of Don's lips suddenly
being replaced by the dirt on her hands.
She says, A struggle then, a struggle.

Victims of the Latest Dance Craze

The streamers choking the main arteries
Of downtown.
The brass band led by a child
From the home for the happicapped.
The old men
Showing their hair (what's left of it),
The buttons of their shirts
Popping in time
To the salsa flooding out
Of their portable headphones,

And mothers letting their babies
Be held by strangers,
And the bus drivers
Taping over their fare boxes
And willing to give directions.

Is there any reason to mention
All the drinks are on the house?
Thick, adolescent boys
Dismantle their BB guns.

Here is the world (what's left of it),
In brilliant motion,
The oil slick at the curb
Danced into a thousand
Splintered steps.
The bag ladies toss off their
Garments
To reveal wings.

■ ■ ■

"This dance you do," drawls the cop,
"What do you call it?"
We call it scalding the air.
We call it dying with your
Shoes on.

And across the street
The bodies of tramps
Stumble
In a sober language.

And across the street
Shy young girls step behind
Their nameless boyfriends,
Twirling their skirts,

And under an archway
A delivery boy discovers
His body has learned to speak,
And what does this street look like
If not a runway,
A polished wood floor?

From the air,
Insects drawn by the sweat
Alight, when possible,
On the blur
Of torsos.
It is the ride
Of their tiny lives.

The wind that burns their wings,
The heaving, oblivious flesh,
Mountains stuffed with panic,
An ocean
That can't make up its mind.

They drop away
With the scorched taste
Of vertigo.

And under a swinging light bulb
Some children
Invent a game
With the shadow the bulb makes
And the beat of their hearts.
They call it dust in the mouth.
They call it horse with no rider.
They call it school with empty books.

In the next room
Their mother throws her dress away to chance.
It drops to the floor
Like a brush sighs across a drum head,
And when she takes her lover,
What are they thinking of
If not a ballroom filled with mirrors,
A world where no one has the right
To stumble?

In a parking lot
An old man says this:
"I am a ghost dance.
I remember the way my hair felt,
Damp with sweat and wind.

When the wind kisses the leaves, I am dancing.
When the subway hits the third rail, I am dancing.
When the barrel goes over Niagara Falls, I am dancing.
Music rings my bones like metal.

■ ■ ■

O, Jazz has come from heaven," he says,
And at the z he jumps, arcing his back like a heron's neck,
And stands suddenly revealed
As a balance demon,
A home for
Stetson hats.

We have all caught the itch:
The neon artist
Wiring up his legs,
The tourist couple
Recording the twist on their
Instamatic camera,
And in a factory,
A janitor asks his broom
For a waltz,
And he grasps it like a woman
He'd have to live another
Life to meet,
And he spins around the dust bin
And machines and thinks:
Is everybody happy?
And he spins out the side door,
Avoiding the cracks in the sidewalk,
Grinning as if he'd just received
The deepest kiss in the world.

Jazz Dancer

I have a theory about motion.
I have a theory about the air.
I have a theory about main arteries and bass lines.
I have theory about Friday night,
Just a theory, mind you,
About a dry mouth and certain kinds of thirst
And a once-a-month bulge of money
   in a working pair of pants.

I have a theory about kisses,
The way a woman draws a man across a dance floor
Like a ship approaching a new world.
I have a theory about space
And what's between the space

And an idea about words,
A theory about balance and the alphabet,
A theory concerning electricity and the tendons,
A hunch about long glances from across a ballroom
Even though there's a man on her arm,
Even though there's a woman on his arm

And Fire and the Ocean,
Stars and Earthquakes,
Explosions as sharp as new clothes
   off the rack.
When I leap,

■ ■ ■

Brushes strike the lip of a cymbal.
When I leap,
A note cuts through glass.
When I leap,

A thick finger dreams on a bass string
And all that sweat,
All that spittle,
All those cigarettes and cheap liquor,

All that lighthearted sass and volcanism,
All that volatile lipstick,
All that

Cleaves the air like a man and woman
Sweet-talk in a bed.
When I leap
I briefly see the world as it is
And as it should be

And the street where I grew up,
The saxophones,
Kisses
And mysteries among the houses

And my sister dressing in front of her mirror,
A secret weapon of sound and motion,
A missionary
In the war against
The obvious.

MARTIN EDMUNDS

Cabin Site,
Christmas Island, N.S.

1.
Where three eagles cross in the sky
a dark shuttle flies
through the long afternoons.

Where three eagles cross in the sky
bury a bone
in the dark.

Where three eagles cross in the sky
a tooth
grinds on stone.

2.
The thudding Atlantic
under rain; spine
of hills through fog.

Ashes from the fire provide
the leavening for bread.
By sputtering candles
the small bodies
of the animals you've killed
do a quick dance
in the black pot, reduce
to a thick, grey stew.

■ ■ ■

Nights when the gloom lifts,
the cloud that hangs in the sky
pours its black milk on the land.
You call your first-born "Moon."

His teeth dig in.
You live off the pain
that lives off you, knowing
from generation
to generation, this
is what survives.

3.
Eyes
in the evening fire;
and today, pinned cruciform
on the sky an eagle:
two plies of darkness,
red-jeweled talons, blood on the wing.

Piri, you lean closer
to the squalling of the crows:

an eye that is a mouth,
a heart all hunger.

Jonathan Lazarus Wright, 1702–1729, from fever after falling in a well

I saw trees walking upside down across
Small Hill, the stone spires reared to toss
black gravel by the handful down the well
and make the water bubble. My hands swell
like breaddough under linen on a sideboard
where shadows whisper, the banked firecoals hiss
and squint into the smoke for Lazarus
who passed his sister, stitching, when he fell.
"Four days he's lain there, Lazarus will smell. . . ."
I smell her throat raw from crying. Lord,
don't let them hold my head up to the damp
beards of elders while the rainclouds tap
white canes against the door to be let in
and someone curses, fumbling with a lamp.
Let the barber take a razor to my chin.
The housedogs, wakened from their evening nap,
growl just the way that sets each other off
like yawning during Sermon, the first cough
which Father likened to original sin.
Faces dissolve like bread on water when
we fished for minnows with a common pin,
the millwheel creaking, the tailrace foaming brown
as bock beer sloshed from hogsheads that time the Crown
and Anchor's publican was whipped through town.
Hope noses my hand open, her puppies sniff,
snort, claw the pineboards, whine, slink back to lick
the poison oozing from my blistered feet
like lambfat dripping onto blackened brick.
A great bird flaps above me, a white sheet
is lowered to lift me skyward in a sling.
Christ butterflies a bent nail to a string.

One for the Road

A dusk so dark woodsmoke
is a hung net unkinking
until the sky opens
a scar of lightning,
forked road down which
a white-faced convict
looks back but comes stumbling.

Claws scrape at the cracked flags
lining the drive.
Red eyes seen through
the steam of its breathing,
sniffing me out.

Let it be.
Let what is leashed
and beaten in me
come and go begging
through the night, lifting
house after house,
city by city,
a torn silence, the bloody
pads of its paws.

At the eye of the storm,
unbearable calm.

Far down the evening,
a dog barks.

Just like that, a man
opens his throat to the moon.

Egypt*

A lapis sky. No moon. The evening stars,
Venus in the southwest,
reddish Mars,
Nut's hennaed nipples, the left one wet with milk.
I have sucked them. I shall never die!

*Nut is the ancient Egyptian sky goddess. Her name rhymes with "root."

A Date with Robbe-Grillet

What I remember didn't happen.
Birds stuttering.
Torches huddled together.
The café empty, with no place to sit.

Birds stuttering.
On our ride in the country
the café empty, with no place to sit.
Your hair was like a doll's.

On our ride in the country
it was winter.
Your hair was like a doll's
and when we met it was as children.

It was winter
when it rained
and when we met it was as children.
You, for example, made a lovely girl.

When it rained
the sky turned the color of pernod.
You, for example, made a lovely girl.
Birds strutted.

The sky turned the color of pernod.
Within the forest
birds strutted
and we came upon a second forest

■ ■ ■

within the forest
identical to the first.
And we came upon a second forest
where I was alone

identical to the first
only smaller and without music
where I was alone
where I alone could tell the story.

Martha Graham

1.
In 1923
for the Greenwich
Village Follies

you performed
three dances
one Oriental
one Moorish

and one
with a large veil.

You said:
"Grace is your
relationship
to the world"

a deep-rooted
inclination
to converse

and just as poetry
is not about words
nor math about numbers

so too the dance
is not about its steps.

2.

With your spooky
Franz Kline makeup
and adolescence
of Indian maidens

the daughter
of Dr. George Graham
a specialist
in nervous disease

you dance
not with lyrical hands
but with
the nervous system

capricious and sterile
as a guillotine
for swans

dark fins
circling the white
of the eyeball.

When the Moon Is Full

It's not unusual
for the face
to fill with fluid
or the hair
carelessly pinned
to grow wet.
When the moon is full
we often dream
that the dead
are back among us
and dying again.

Aleister Crowley Slept Here

There is something banal about evil
but the reverse is also true
and what is mundane quickly becomes sinister.
Like the building on the corner
where his ghost tampers with a geranium.
So ordinary yet gloomy,
one senses he was bored
and this can be verified
in his autobiography, wherein he states,
"I confess to dislike Chicago . . .
It gives the impression of being a pure machine."
Of his apartment, there is not much to see.
A Weber grill, pale yellow and never used
that the new tenants installed on the balcony.
If I meet them, I will ask
if they have nightmares often
although it is not likely.
He was older when he resided here.
Pretty much the retired Prospero
who'd broken his wand in favor of literature.
A mistake, in this city, as he found out
when calling on the editor of *Poetry Magazine*.
A poetess, of whom he writes,
"I am still not sure if she knew my name
and my work, but she showed no interest whatsoever!"
As you see, things haven't changed.
I live down the street
and often he haunts the neighborhood
searching, as I am, for this or that line.
And after storms I always think
those knots of wet string
you find coiled on the sidewalk
must surely have belonged to him.

You Go to My Head

The outcome was
unexpected
             a light and silly note
             on the table
after rowing like a galley slave
to open the bronze door
             and still in my
"journey to the center of the earth"
             rags,
I come home to find
such music as I've never heard pour
from the dolphin-headed faucets.
It's just that I had pictured
something more dramatic
             than a cocktail.
Who thinks of such things
             in a gloomy old cave?
"But my dear," you said
winding a towel around your head.
"It doesn't take a genie
to see you're destined
             for fun
and awful as it sounds
you must learn to make the best of it."

MARTÍN ESPADA

Tiburón

East 116th
and a long red car
stalled with the hood up
roaring salsa
like a prize shark
mouth yanked open
and down in the stomach
the radio
of the last fisherman
still tuned
to his lucky station

Voodoo Cucumbers

He was Haitian too,
but he was Doc Hunt's crewleader:
everybody called him 99
because he kept the Haitian crews
working with voodoo power,
picking Maryland crops hands adrenalin-driven
by 99 double-number bad magic.

They wouldn't leave without him.
The Haitian crews, some marooned
by the shipwreck of used cars
paid for with no English
in the next town,
others shouting and slamming dominoes
on the common table,
betting postponed wages
in front of the satan-hot metal shacks.
Immigration papers say
Entry Without Inspection,
Deportable.
Two weeks gone
waiting for work,
waiting for 99,
they could pick peaches west of here.
They won't leave without him.

This is Doc Hunt's trade:
99's crews pick voodoo cucumbers
and cursed tomatoes
weathered at roadside stands,
cellophaned at supermarkets,
sold for salad.

The Right Hand of a Mexican Farmworker in Somerset County, Maryland

A rosary tattoo
between thumb
and forefinger
means that
every handful
of crops and dirt
is a prayer,
means that Christ
had hard hands
too

The Policeman's Ball

It was
a policeman's ball,
old-timey cop stomp
polka kept the beat
with a boot blood-spotted
and a hand that clapped,
so that after the dance
the suspect couldn't
snap his fingers

Boot Camp Incantation

Marine base, Quantico, Virginia, 1977

What does a Marine feel
when he kills the enemy?

The recoil of his M-16.

From an Island You Cannot Name

Thirty years ago,
your linen-gowned father stood
in the dayroom of the VA hospital,
grabbing at the plastic
identification bracelet
marked Negro,
shouting "I'm not!
Take it off!
I'm Other!"

The army photograph
pinned to your mirror
says he was,
black, Negro,
dark as West Indian rum.

And this morning,
daughter of a man
from an island you cannot name,
you gasp tears
trying to explain
that you're Other,
that you're not.

KATHY FAGAN

The Raft

Walking this inland city under rain there are
so few elements that speak to us of home:
a tall potted flower on a neighboring porch,
red as a Spanish dancer and as liable
to spin where she stands; or the trees we have
learned to call catalpa, which means
"head with wings," their bean pods surging
down the deep gutter rapids of our street.
No wonder we stand on the hard pocked shore
of the lake tonight, lonely for oceans we've lived by.
Solitary, but for the scavenging stars and the one
low cloud that is our ghost ship. Turn from it,
love, and lie with me. On the soft surf
of our breath we go, a small raft, a sleeping oarsman,
out from a harbor the odor of loss,
the odor of a woman, looking back.

Desire

How the melody of a single ice cream truck
can rise from the streets of your city
and bring with it every year you have ever known.
How it can bring forth children
and the promise that has always belonged to them
and the shining dimes and the rush of icy vapors
from the truck's freezer to the sky.
How it rises past the green froth of maple leaves
to your window as if to say, *Summer already,*
here for you and haven't they always been?
And haven't you given each one of them away,
your arms lifted, your mouth opened
for the cool winds of October?
Yes, you think, on the other side of the country
in the long tanned valleys of California,
the fiddle-neck curls upon itself and crows pull
every living morsel from the soft ground.
And farther west, on the warming coastal rocks
of the Pacific, crabs raise their one good arm
to the sun—like the farmer in China you imagine
or the dusty pistils of tulips in Europe. But you
have to be here, listening to an incessant song and children
who want, who want, no more and no less than yourself.
Tell your sorrow to the gulls that flail outside
your window, too far inland for their own good.
They could be at any shore but they are here
and isn't that all they're good for:
to be screamed at, to scream back?
Tell it to the man who shares your bed
and he will weight his head more deeply
into his pillow, touching your hand out of habit,
taking you ever farther from the life you wanted
as if you ever wanted a life, as if your many mounting desires
led to no more than the final consolation of silence

and the long dreamless sleep of those who hunger for nothing.
That is the lie we tell ourselves—that we can do without
this life. For if night darkened our eyes and our very hearts
turned cold as the moon, then wouldn't you
take it all back if you could? Three thin dimes in your pocket
and the music of a truck close to your ear and the summer
already moist in your armpits—don't you want to wrap your lips
around the melting sweetness of it? Won't you pay
and keep paying for as long as you must, to know
it belongs, has always belonged, to you?

An excerpt from
Five Nights in the North Country

. . . nothing which has once been formed can perish . . .
                                                                    —Freud

SOLSTICE
There was a sound of grouse from the field
    of grouse or a box guitar
And the way the storm idled over the mountain
    revealing the mountain   dissolving in light
Was the way the grouse and the rubbery strumming
    advanced and withdrew across the field
Crossing it thereby   not on the wind
    but on the driest memory of their own first making
And that is why fireflies startled from place
    from their daytime places in the weeds and grass
Resembled the words of a child's Vocabulary
    their lessons divulged   their lessons concealed
And to the child for whom a word yields meaning
    one word that emerges apart from its fellows
To unroll its syllables   suddenly   everywhere
    it is repetition that implies urgency
And urgent repetition that doubts it away
    like the triad of firefly beats on a screen
Green as the silver of lime in a glass
    that lit the ice   that lit the lamp
By which the dark seemed gladly dazzled
    sure as it was of some enormity of its own
Elsewhere   and not far   from here

An excerpt from
Five Poems of Farewell

THE LIT STATIONS

I know now when I walk over subway grates
my shadow enters the station before me.
I have seen others break the railed light
and the thin lines of spring rain that flow there.

And when the train sounds its harsh iambs of approach,
sweeping my hair and my clothes and the sharp odor of rot all
                                                    around me,

I am grateful.

The doors slide apart for me.
I choose a seat before a window,
my feet surrounded by the torn petals of a carnation.

I read ads in the language I have begun to dream in.

And in the tunnel of darkness, there is the skeleton of my face.

And in the lit stations, the white tiles of my cared-for childhood.

14. 23. 28.

I have committed them to heart, ivory and ornate
within the chalk-blue corners
and draped in the robes of the Virgin.

■ ■ ■

Passengers in raincoats hold down their laps,
stare at scraps of news boot-pasted to the floor.

It could be 1914, Voulangis, France,
the Steichen photograph of *Heavy Roses:*
each brown and weary and obstinate,
each instinctively knowing his terminus.

Letter to My Mother

"Goodbye" is not quite true; we'll meet tonight
as we do at night, in various disguises
through acres of dreams, though in another country
you cook alone and riffle through the bills.
When I tongue the envelope to seal it
I see the two of us, the year we slept
together, my mouth rose around your breast.
These thin sheets I write on aren't so different
from those that covered us: insubstantial,
vulnerable to wind, to sudden tearing.

Each woman keeps a secret: that her first love
was a woman, even if she later turned
to others. Now the pleasure of a bowl
of cherries, still warm from the tree, is never
far from danger; if I burst the fruit against
my teeth, recklessly, over and over,
your body may rise up, first food, first pleasure,
naming all the others imitations,
claiming me, sealing my mouth over
with yours, the kiss I dream about and dread.

I made my mind up early on that you
would be more independent than I was—
instead you gave the package you'd been given:
bottles, useless matches, chips of sobs,
all broken, like a lamp sent through the mail.
Here where I am the box holds only letters.
But even here, where the language I must speak
is not the one I learned from you, the landscape
daily touches deeper, olives bend
over the mountain, cypress grips the steep

■ ■ ■

embankment, and the more I look I love.
Every helpless time your voice is with me,
your skin, your smells, the beating of your heart.
I can't help thinking you would be more happy
if you could forget—your anger, pounded
flat, like foil hung among the cherries
to scare the birds, has beauty of its own.
When the south wind strips leaves from the plane trees
every gust is your unspoken wanting:
hot, strong, pitilessly dry.

I want hills blanked in snow, all sound muffled,
still and cold, colorless, to soothe
the upsurge of angry love and sadness
your letter brings. Everywhere I go
since first leaving you I am the lover
who celebrates and heals. You taught me. Now
you're my only failure: hunched with morning
coffee, or at night hollowed by work,
then hammered into sleep. My exiled power
comes to nothing: the bite of postmarks, ink.

The International Meteorological Committee Reports

The Pripyat River flows on, we assure you.
The cattle lying down in the cars
of the trains into Poland are probably tired.
We also are tired. Generally
we are held responsible only
for crop failures and the ruin of outdoor commencements.
Suddenly we are the angels who hold
the four winds of the earth. Suddenly we're up day and night,
soothing the press, placating the public,
watching the needles of our instruments.

In summer, when it's fine, we in Mikolajki
take a regional pride in our breezes.
We see no reason now to attack
an old friend over some spoiled lettuce
or the loss of a few reindeer in the north.
Of course we've shipped the children to camps
and limited their outdoor play to two hours.
For them it's summer holidays early. For us,
the lack of milk is no sacrifice;
the winds are strong drink, reserved for adults.

Yes, the fire is still smoking; frankly
we in Los Angeles can't help but admire
its purposefulness, how it has resisted
the volunteer fireboys' airdrops of boron
and sand. The Helsinki panel concurs;
that tail of harnessed sun belongs
to all of us, as humans; all
should share in the parental boasting.
Now, we admit, it strains our patience,
but so originally, with such splendor.

■ ■ ■

Off the record, the Nice branch finds it flattering
how this iodine enters the body, like a lover,
finds the secret place that is its alone
and nestles there, dividing, forever.
Yes, the Vilnius committee regrets
we've lost two citizens so far, but
one can't run from endings; after all,
less than twenty years of our century remain.
What's essential is to leave our mark;
and who can ever forget us now?

The plants along the Pripyat
will bloom shovel leaves, the lizard's tail
bisect, the forks of the serpent's tongue
join, the rocks themselves will pulse
the ardent, invisible heat we provided
and the children of Prague and Budapest
and perhaps even Belfast, Boston, Beijing,
long after our gravestones are broken to shivers
will for generations learn to repeat:
Chernobyl Chernobyl Chernobyl.

—May 1986

MARTHA HOLLANDER

The Detective Examines the Body

Nothing but an assemblage
of cylinders, it rests
on the sidewalk at dawn.
He sees it easily enough
as the crowd parts,
giving him shy looks
and shuffling back as if
unveiling a monument.
Only a few minutes later
the police come by
to draw a white outline
around the important corpse
before spiriting it away.
Still, the world that is
or was the person
shimmers uneasily at him,
in the blank frame
that waves at nothing
(one arm up, one leg bent)
like an exuberant bit
of graffiti. Stenciled
on the damp ground,
it's as pure and inviting
as a footprint: he's
ready to hurl himself
into the mold
and test the fit.

But there's work to do
among those living
organisms called suspects.
With each visit he returns
to the body's volumes

and superb angles, bones
darting forward, skin and fat
swimming sexily over them.
Calibrated to arouse
and astound, to inspire,
to warn, the real thing
hums with life and language:
hip and shoulder, waist
allied with knee, strike
the room's four walls
like an epiphany. Each
possession there becomes
an extra limb, a bright
icon of motive saluting
his eye and hand. (His own
body, like his beliefs, is
hidden behind the usual
trenchcoat.) It's enough
to take in the books, the bed,
scarves and scribbled notes,
a large ashtray that he
suddenly picks up

and then to sit silently,
alone. Like the smoke
from his innumerable
cigarettes, facts hover
in a probable fog.
What they all call
the science of deduction
comes down to one simple rule:
The body is the sole truth.
Beginning with the morning
silhouette, he moves on
to shadows burned into
the streets of destroyed
cities. Whole beings have been
reduced to light in a hideous

reversal: matter made thought.
The murdered soul wanders
nowhere, instead is trapped
in a chalk shape. He's sure
that if he put an ear to cold
concrete, he'd hear someone
wailing to be let out, like
the princess in the Chinese
myth of echo who fell
into a vat of molten bronze
and was cast as a bell.

So the case (what a word
for that jangling mass
of brutality and doubt)
will be stubbornly put
through its paces
until the terrible
unmaking is unmasked.
As thought once more
becomes matter, the body
can be brought alarmingly
to life: this is the mystery.
Manners and money, the love
borne for another, must be
reinvented from that solitary
bit of flesh. As if eyeing it
up and down, he moves from
the shell of the victim to
the fierce pulse of survival.
For the living are infected
by oblivion, always on
the brink of falling into its
heady company. Whoever did it
will, in time, be seduced,
alone, unable to bear it
now that the dead have left
their inescapable, empty mark.

Ogata Kōrin on His Field of Irises

Kyoto, c. 1701

Neither you nor I would imagine gardens
    like this, but my tacit brush
    sees differently. On the
folding screen that will invent a fresh young room
    with the stern economy
    of a knife, there arises
a company of irises and sweeping
    blades of leaf. They explode from
    gold ground (not earth but ether,
that sumptuous nothingness which the flat world
    so disrupts) as if growing
    miraculously from sand.
Descending in a skittish diagonal
    they stumble a bit, but then
    it's you who must be stumbling
in this burning gold envelope of summer.
    your head lolls along with the
    plushy tip of each flower
as if you had laced their scent with your *sake*.
    Now we both know they might be
    calligraphy after all,
delicious ideograms in just two styles
    of purple, and the poem
    encoded in their nodding
petals will speak no louder than a whisper.
    Three homesick gentlemen stopped
    to weep at the eight-fold bridge
overgrown with irises. Inspired by grief,
    they composed an acrostic
    lament on the syllables
of iris, more a sigh than a word, really,

in pale English: to the left
all disappears off the edge
only to start again, in the following
panel, with a few opaque
stalks, like a voice rising in
gentle inquiry as it murmurs *iris*.
The garrulous right-hand screen,
though, whose chatter of blossoms
peaks and ebbs as they scallop across the air
with the eager precision
of architectural bays,
will only answer with *kakitsubata*:
The drawn-out stutter of sobs
like those of the courtiers,
choking with sentiment and poetizing,
who cried until their lunch of
dried rice was dampened with tears.

I paint, naturally, for money. What can
summon all this eloquent
growth as urgently as gain?
On the other hand, you might say that I paint
money itself, that the gold
medium where nature springs
is every coin ever coveted, now ground
to powder and sprinkled on
the waiting screen, now warming
and at last melting happily in the sun.
Wealth, like a rare essence, can
flower from the minimal.
Soothing the rich, my resonant irises
are still richer themselves: for
look how simply they bestow
a lush nostalgia on the chamber where you
make love, make tea, give or take
counsel! Real privilege is
what we mean by art, where the satisfaction

you seek effortlessly bears
you up with the elegant
starkness of purple, green, gold. Each unadorned
leaf startles with intent, like
a woman's bright wrist and knee
parting her kimono as she leans forward
to hand me a new iris
of my own. Tearing apart
the petals I observe once more how painting
reduces truth. What we make
from nothing need only be
enough for recognition: the audacious
colors conceived on precious
metal, no eight-fold bridge, no
time, place, tears. These are already among your
luxurious possessions
which, in the old days, were quite
understood—and how I'd welcome a signal
from the lean past in these hot,
bedizened days, from what our
weak emperors have lost! Here, only here, is
the flower of that court, with
its pleasure and clarity
and with its sorrowing gentlemen poets,
a material world of
things left glowingly unsaid.

Back in the Twilight Zone

for David Leavitt

In the television's pale square of light
there stretches a paler desert, small town
skirted by the loneliest of mountains,
or the hot surface of an asteroid.
Wherever it is, it's summer, always
and ever after, flooding this landscape
of fear with its bright, banal deception.
Soon a hapless man will wander into
the frame and try to feel at home, looking
for a sign, a telephone pole, footprints.
Perhaps this is the world after the bomb
and he the final astronaut, alone
and uncomprehending; in any case
those who constantly watch him will know first.

In the evening grasses of New England
a boy sits upright and recognizes
traffic, shouts, and church bells. He remembers
being driven through the desert, frightened
even by the serene forks of cactus
that guarded the immense family car.
For there was death in the open, not caught
for a crazy instant in the dread eyes
of buffalo skulls (as a camera
would have it), but glaring eternally,
just as day frowns on a parched asteroid.
He dreamed he found a pair of glasses there
with hypnotic powers. They were throwing
gleams on the already gleaming dust, like
sunlight piercing a television screen
with fiercer reflection.

■ ■ ■

In a small hot lens every place becomes
empty of events. The boy knows of this
from staring at deserts on the late show,
where the known horizon disappears
in a blinding concavity of sky.
He takes off his own innocent glasses:
his eyes are edged with mauve shadows, as if
bruised by what they saw out there in the sand,
what lost aliens and astronauts saw.
And like the damp grass clinging to his skin,
like the first prickle of disease, he feels
a sudden enormous silence switch on
that can only mean someone is watching.

Maquillage

After nestling champagne splits in ice
I'd line the bottles behind the bar. Tapped,
they made a chilly music, *an arsenal*
of bells you called it. When I circled my arms
around myself I could count ribs
under my cotton shift. Rochelle sat at the stage's
edge warming her satin costume. She
couldn't bear the cold cloth. On the way
to your rooms I'd adjust blue lights for her.

René, that year you were the only father
I'd admit. Before opening each evening
we'd sip wine coolers on the balcony,
watch the day burn out over the square
and fountain with its cluster of stone cherubs.

With a straight razor you'd shave your face,
clean, then smooth indigo on your lids
and draw the lines of your mouth. Nights
you shook too much I'd do your face,
the wig, make you talk. It became a way
of managing the days, evening's slow descent
until the city turned in its fever
and music rose through the floor.

I'd serve while Rochelle balanced
on a sequinned ball, stepping down
to the blown sound of blues. She'd gyrate
till she'd lost it all and you'd glide, joking
among tables, benevolent in a rayon kimono.
All night the river of men swerved
under their solitary stars, and we'd go on,

■ ■ ■

minor players waking startled to the care
or harm of such unlikely hands, surprised
to hit the lights and find the place
so shabby: numbers on the wall, the butts
and broken glass. Quiet long after closing,
I'd lean by the door and smoke, hear
the fountain erode those cherubs' faces.

You're nowhere I know anymore, René.
The future we predicted is the past
and different. You're the empty room
morning pours into through a torn shade,
that place you said most nearly spells peace
in the heart, narrow glasses on the ledge
reflecting the horizon.

Tonight, children's quarreling rises
from the yard. For a moment, through shutters
the city relights itself until it's time
for music to shiver the floorboards,
the hour of plumage . . .

But that was long ago. I was only seventeen.

Chinese New Year

The dragon is in the street dancing beneath windows
    pasted with colored squares, past the man
who leans into the phone booth's red pagoda, past
    crates of doves and roosters veiled

until dawn. Fireworks complicate the streets
    with sulphur as people exchange gold
and silver foil, money to appease ghosts
    who linger, needy even in death. I am

almost invisible. Hands could pass through me
    effortlessly. This is how it is
to be so alien that my name falls from me, grows
    untranslatable as the shop signs,

the odors of ginseng and black fungus that idle
    in the stairwell, the corridor where
the doors are blue mouths ajar. Hands
    gesture in the smoke, the partial moon

of a face. For hours the soft numeric
    click of mah-jongg tiles drifts
down the hallway where languid Mai trails
    her musk of sex and narcotics.

There is no grief in this, only the old year
    consuming itself, the door knob blazing
in my hand beneath the light bulb's electric jewel.
    Between voices and fireworks

■ ■ ■

wind works bricks to dust—*hush, hush*—
   no language I want to learn. I can touch
the sill worn by hands I'll never know
   in this room with its low table

where I brew chrysanthemum tea. The sign
   for Jade Palace sheds green corollas
on the floor. It's dangerous to stand here
   in the chastening glow, darkening

my eyes in the mirror with the gulf of the rest
   of my life widening away from me, waiting
for the man I married to pass beneath
   the sign of the building, to climb

the five flights and say his Chinese name for me.
   He'll rise up out of the puzzling streets
where men pass bottles of rice liquor, where
   the new year is liquor, the black bottle

the whole district is waiting for, like
   some benevolent arrest—the moment
when men and women turn to each other and dissolve
   each bad bet, every sly mischance,

the dalliance of hands. They turn in lamplight
   the way I turn now. Wai Min is in the doorway.
He brings fish. He brings lotus root.
   He brings me ghost money.

Jackson Hotel

Sometimes after hours of wine I can almost see
   the night gliding in low off the harbor
      down the long avenues of shop windows

past mannequins, perfect in their gestures.
   I leave water steaming on the gas ring
      and sometimes I can slip from my body,

almost find the single word to prevent evenings
   that absolve nothing, a winter lived alone
      and cold. Rooms where you somehow marry

the losses of strangers that tremble
   on the walls like the hands
      of the dancer next door, luminous

with Methedrine, she taps walls for hours
   murmuring about the silver she swears
      lines the building, the hallways

where each night drunks stammer their
   usual rosary until they come to rest
      beneath the tarnished numbers, the bulbs

that star each ceiling.
   I must tell you I am afraid to sit here
      losing myself to the hour's cold erasure

■ ■ ■

until I know myself only by this cold weight,
    this hand on my lap, palm up.
        I want to still the dancer's hands

in mine, to talk about forgiveness
    and what we leave behind—faces
        and cities, the small emergencies

of nights. I say nothing, but
    leaning on the sill, I watch her leave
        at that moment

when the first taxis start rolling
    to the lights of Chinatown, powered
        by sad and human desire. I watch her fade

down the street until she's a smudge,
    violet in the circle of my breath. A figure
        so small I could cup her in my hands.

Black Mare

It snakes behind me, this invisible chain gang—
the aliases, your many faces peopling

that vast hotel, the past. What did we learn?
Every twenty minutes the elevated train,

the world shuddering beyond
the pane. It was never warm enough in winter.

The walls peeled, the color of corsages
ruined in the air. Sweeping the floor,

my black wig on the chair. I never meant
to leave you in that hotel where the voices

of patrons long gone seemed to echo in the halls,
a scent of spoiled orchids. But this was never

an elegant hotel. The iron fretwork of the El
held each room in a deep corrosive bloom.

This was the bankrupt's last chance, the place
the gambler waits to learn his black mare's

leg snapped as she hurtled towards the finish line.

■

How did we live? Your face over my shoulder
was the shade of mahogony in the speckled

mirror bolted to the wall. It was never warm.
You arrived through a forest of needles,

the white mist of morphine, names for sleep
that never came. My black wig unfurled

across the battered chair. Your arms circled
me when I stood by the window. Downstairs

the clerk who read our palms broke the seal
on another deck of cards. She said you're my fate,

my sweet annihilating angel, every naked hotel room
I've ever checked out of. There's nothing

left of that, but even now when night pulls up
like a limousine, sea-blue, and I'm climbing the stairs,

keys in hand, I'll reach the landing and
you're there—the one lesson I never get right.

Trains hurtled by, extinguished somewhere
past the bend of midnight. The shuddering world.

Your arms around my waist. I never meant to leave.

■

Of all of that, there's nothing left but a grid
of shadows the El tracks throw over the street,

the empty lot. Gone, the blistered sills
voices that rilled across each wall. Gone,

the naked bulb swinging from the ceiling,
that chicanery of light that made your face

a brief eclipse over mine. How did we live?
The mare broke down. I was your fate, that

yellow train, the plot of sleet through dust
crusted on the pane. It wasn't warm enough.

What did we learn? All I have left of you
is this burnt place on my arm. So, I won't

forget you even when I'm nothing but
small change in the desk clerk's palm, nothing

but the pawn ticket crumpled in your pocket,
the one you'll never redeem. Whatever I meant

to say loses itself in the bend of winter
towards extinction, this passion of shadows falling

like black orchids through the air. I never meant
to leave you there by the pane, that

terminal hotel, the world shuddering with trains.

Goodbye

Upstairs, a man is writing a screenplay about assassins
Who shrink to the size of pills and travel the pipes and drains

Of our city, from embassy to embassy, extinguishing conflicts.
A hope, I suppose, derived from evenings soaking alone in a tub.

Downstairs, a solemn pair residents call *the flesh eaters* pack and go,
Taking their notorious dog, who howled ballads from Hell.

I find myself on the stoop explaining your death to an eight-year-old
Who's been storing your favorite ice cream in her freezer for weeks.

"But how will he come back?" she asks, mildly annoyed.
The sad insufficiencies of transportation drop clues all around us . . .

Not subways. Not planes. Not trucks nuzzling fenders near the emeralds
And rubies of traffic lights. Not buses, those elephants

Of the New World, toting the moderately intrepid like pangs of emotion,
Their sides plastered with advice.

Poor you if you've wound up in some ethereal jungle.
But, then again, poor you if Heaven is too much like what we already know:

A roadless place on a map of dust where everything vanishes without
Explanation—the capital I of your body laid out beneath

■ ■ ■

The uninformed chatter of leaves, cloth of your skin unweaving,
Tumbled poles of your bones, no longer animated argument of your lungs

Merely a fragrance now, and soon not even that.
Better that you go where perfect sentences take up the letters

Of your name, and the agonizing softness of what was once your weight
Becomes the tint of your unhurried soul,

While here professors of dread and remorse speak of you
Endlessly, by heart.

Tulips: A Selected History

On your street, whose name means "roundabout" in Dutch,
The mildest weather conditions vibrate the spines of your neighbors,
Who gamble on the tulip market losing fortunes.

One gauges the sun like a bank account.
Another tastes the soils of everyone's front yards
While his dinner grows cold.

But for you the rain has come to sound like
The dead gossiping about the dead, and you warm yourself with
The thought that evening and its underpinnings impales them all

Sooner or later, through the windows of their neat homes,
While they wake or sleep in the same chair, at odd hours,
Mistaking physical pain for desire.

It is the sort of night when the sky seems about to reveal its secrets.
Your wife stirs soup outdoors under the moon,
The not-so-dear orchids of garlic steaming.

She sips from an iron spoon reflecting clouds and pretends
It is a broth of your priceless Tulipa, her dowry all spent
On seedlings and bulbs, drawers of fragrant possibility,

A rich man's drying room, and flower beds. She envisions
The wives of tulipomaniacs in Portugal, their swarthy, faceless
Husbands lugging home large bouquets of glorious colorations,

■ ■ ■

Unimaginable forms. This would needle you, of course,
But the thing to remember about women and cooking is that they do it,
As they do all things, for love.

When she frowns, as she does now,
When she looks wearily down the path where two cows are lowing
As darkness circles and drops,

It is not the chore that tires her
But the relentless composting between the sweat of the real world
And the ravage of the one she would make for you if she could,

Out of moon, out of water, out of whatever has gone wrong,
Never knowing it was a dream you wanted,
And that you had it all along.

Police Sift New Clues in Search for Beauty
—headline in the Post

Outside the precinct, the continents sway
In a monster wind.

A cat snoozes on a humidifier
In the corner of the squad room,

Its unfettered breath keeping time
With the office clock.

Her favorite cop glares at
The barracuda faces of wanted men

Posted in a row on the wall, their beauty
Clearly drained off, but to where?

"I did it and I'm glad," says the first face.
"I did it and I'm glad," says the next.

The Public Defender chews his lunch thoughtfully,
As if feeling for nails with his teeth.

All morning and afternoon,
He and the rookies plowed through fields

Of bluish data on the old gunmetal desk,
Each in his own way.

The P.D. has fears of dying, of rescuing
A maiden who crushes him with her weight and terror.

■ ■ ■

He keeps one eye on the door,
The pale glue of a tear idling beneath his lid.

Through the glass partition
To the captain's office, someone mutters

"I know it's here somewhere . . .
I saw it, for Chrissake!"

Slowly, against the breakers,
Evening sets sail on the East River,

With its freight of passions,
As, uptown in Helsinki, her evidence

Burning gaily in the handsome fireplace,
Beauty reads her mail.

And in Caracas
Beauty plunges her hand into a book

As if to read it by touch.
And in a murky corner of Antwerp

Beauty unwraps
A heart-round box of chocolates,

Each one the dark shape of a hill.
And in Irkutsk

Beauty, bending to tie a shoe,
Lifts up her head expectantly.

Glass

At 8 P.M., each office window
Is a propped-up laboratory slide from the Mad Scientist's files.

Slide A reveals a janitor who studies the dark in a doorway,
Slide B a clutter of memos folded into hats, and there

An executive hopeful nearly lost in fluorescent smudge,
Who plods late into the evening, alone, for little pay—

It's Mr. X of the Department for Redundancy Department,
Another pheasant under glass for the gods.

Gray angels nibble on his window ledge—ornithology knocking
On the door of evolution—and as he reaches to pet them

His hand flattens instead on that first page of the intangible,
That portrait of physics buried in the transparent.

WAYNE KOESTENBAUM

Shéhérazade

1. ASIE

One word, "nacreous,"
coils in me like a conch, a minaret,
or a question always in the process of being posed.
    My favorite part's *comme un*
immense oiseau de nuit, my bedtimes
moor in that glissando, even
    if I've planned a future
that gives no love affairs
    no berth, a future stuck in its circuit like a sun. *Perse*

    ou Chine are nice spots
on the map but don't try visiting them,
they will crumble in your fingers like a butterfly's wing.
    Even the felt fez
I bought at MGM's closeout sale
has an aura chalked on its brim:
    1940. I guess
some escapist flick
    wrung forehead-sweat from an extra, discoloring the rim.

    If I kiss the fez
I can almost taste his tribulation.
On my toilet lid sits a fragrant spirit, weak blue, called
    Eau de senteur á l'iris.
When I open it, out comes a djinn
named Shirley: she used to live in
    empty medicine vials
with *contrapposto*
    curve when turned upside down. Can you smell by hearing?
    Asie

■ ■ ■

   smells like the floral
print my aunt wore to the fireworks the year
she died. But I imagine that she took a bargain junket
   and "went native," like Gauguin,
staying in the tropics with a woman
she loved. What I hear enters me,
   Ravel scored it so
the tremor in *voir*
   makes me clench my rectum. In *Chine* it dizzied me to sit

   by the chaperone's
plum pudding embonpoint: she should have been
minding her own daughter, a girl discovering the world
   in the hand of her flutist-
boyfriend unbuttoning her blouse—fjord
in a training bra. I know this
   from legend. That evening
in Shanghai, pleading
   nausea, she kept the audience waiting for a half-hour

   and then never played—
her hands paralyzed as a consequence
of romance. Or had she swallowed poison? Strangely, the girl
   who hadn't played was received
favorably by the Shanghai press, who saw
her lack of "tone color" as one
   flaw in an otherwise
magical evening—
   drifting now away from me. When I cry *Asie, Asie,*

   my own breasts are just
visible below my arm's equator,
for I am Ingres' Odalisque, a jewel, like a spit globe,
   dropping from my ear but seized
by happiness at the latitude
where pain is supposed to begin,

and staying there forever,
slave to a moment's
    dream that land is liquid, that there's no prime
        meridian.

2. LA FLÛTE ENCHANTÉE
    A common complaint is that words are not kinetic.
An Egyptian fag
    dangles from the rouged lips
of Reynaldo Hahn—in Proust's bed—
humming "*Si mes vers avaient des ailes.*"
    Nothing I can write will have
such wings. Is there a word in French like "fag"
for cigarettes, or only in the English of Dick Whittington?

    Reynaldo's hair is not more whitened now, there is no
deeper wistfulness
    it can achieve. The art
of sitting still I never learned,
I longed to be the Winged Victory
    seeming to fly but staying
fixed, as slender boys with artistic tastes
molt into husbands, shedding lisps. The dead grandfather

    I never met has a nicotined look in pictures,
as if he were steeped
    in smoke, a black cherry
compote in cordial handed down
for generations. No one eats it,
    but the seersaying sissy
curious about metamorphosis
questions this crystal ball in which a sodden cherry floats,

    he dredges the glass for secrets. To be torn apart
is my ambition,
    not, like Actaeon, limb

by limb, but in a prolonged waltz
of changes, every measure a new
    hiding-place opening up
within me, skin turning to bark, and back
to skin, as when the undressing dark camp counselor in

    our cabin's ochre light turned to me as a painting
is caught by the glance
    of moonlight because the guard,
careless, has left the sash undrawn.
The flaw in primal scenes is that they
    happen, by definition,
only once. When mine happened, I was rapt
with the quest for ladybugs, my eyes on the ground to find

    coordinates of a world threatening to take wing.
My first song, "Frère
    Jacques," made me think our block
was bisected by a slender
ocean—not the song's words, but the song
    itself, the coin it carried
in its purse, convinced me there was a port
two houses down. But I found no harbor, no pirate ship—

    nothing but a front lawn lost in thought. Wouldn't you
run away to catch
    an ocean if it called
and asked for you by your first name—
as if the sea has plans for you, churning
    in memory of what you
do not know lies ahead, a future strange
as the fate of my friend Sue: riding to school, her new flute

■ ■ ■

in the bike's basket, she made too sharp a turn and saw
her flute seem to fly
   willfully from its case
and land beneath a Mack truck's wheel!
Who could play a flute flattened by chance,
   its keys and air holes blended
so that she can't distinguish what is space
from what is silver, what is blank from what the wheel has filled?

3. L'INDIFFÉRENT

Poor Daphne, changed into a laurel. Her lip—
   the lower one—is racked
by cold sores, always will be.
   Without such scars, how could I recognize
her essence? In a Venn diagram
she intersects the Daphne
   Industrial Park near the concert hall.
Why she is linked to an unleased lot, I cannot say,

nor why creepers grow in Eden to this day,
   an alphabet on rocks,
nor why, on a map, I share
   a bruise-colored crosshatched square with Ravel,
or my bandleader Mr. Tristan
overlaps with Yseult's Tristan.
   Praising me, he'd shout, "Good show!" I showed
and showed without pause to his—dare I say girlish?—face,

as if his bandroom were Tangier. He led us
   in a tango so tranced
it tore my life into parts
   like the eye those sisters bicker over—
never long in one socket before
they wrench it out. Poor eye, subject
   to the sisters' quarrels. That is why
antinomies sicken me, and why I prefer slow

■ ■ ■

students to quick ones: I loved the girl whose dream
   was winning a game show
from her living room's eyrie,
   her insights so piercing she needn't
appear in flesh as a contestant.
Angels carried her right answers
   to the TV studio, and coins,
as from a one-armed bandit, flooded her house. I, too,

am guilty of magic carpet rides. "Girlish"
   never refers to girls—
only to boys. It's a vast
   waste of breath to call a girl girlish, a boy
boyish. Why does the word "girlish" age
so inconspicuously, show
   so little tarnish, indifferent
to trends in usage, firm to its troubled course? The page

bleakly shimmers as the girlish boy decides,
   at last, to write his tale
of travel, having never
   crossed the border of his own creation,
the fence around his first disaster.
Twenty years ago, in the deep
   of my life, wondering if I could rise
to a bewilderment greater than age eight, I rode

my bike straight into a man who shouted, "Damn girl,
   watch out where you're going!"
He was drunk—so I reasoned—
   to mistake my sex. I enter the boy
I used to be, who lies in my bed,
naked, as if I've purchased him
   from an Arabian sorceress
who sews the body to its sorrow, invisibly.

The Moving Occupations

after seeing Caravaggio's Bacchus

    Summer light I was driving towards
      Became, up close,
Winter, and at the highway's unexpected
End I shivered and rolled up the windows.
    A minor chord

    Swelled in my car's cathedral.
      I love and fear
The moving occupations: your naked
Realistic throat, Bacchus, and your sneer,
    Flushing you from nipple

    To the hand that lifts a god's wine glass,
      Cannot intend
To invite, but I follow you into the room
Where I want Paul—nearly a stranger, a foreign
    Man I heard get lost

    Traveling through our unresolved
      First conversation
About how Proust lingers on the doorstep
Of sex for hours and never knocks. Motion
    Will not solve

    Destination: into the forest—
      Our human, nervous
Days—or into this dream of a clearing, a bed
I love better than any truthfulness?
    Paul's interest

■ ■ ■

In burning journeys, like a book of prayer
    Put in the pocket
For its weight and not its words, is a cry
I seem to hear out of a deep thicket.
    Our full stare

Falters and goes underground.
    I thought I had
Outgrown wanting to be unsatisfied,
Asking Paul whether the Baroque head
    Weighted down

With leaves is passionate enough,
    If he sees
What I accept, the invitation of pallor,
The room's goblet spilling, hewn drapery
    Slipping off

The shoulder—but the boy's enduring
    Eyes are their own
Luxury, with nothing more to say.
In his indifference I am alone, as the car
    Stammers, journeys

In the difficult direction,
    Turning where the man
Advised not to, following what I know
From boys and fables, not the throats of logicians
    Whose theorems

Are only beautiful when wrong.
    I used to chase
The pretty girls in third grade to the fence
To marry them; my travels have darkened, Bacchus,
    And the girls are gone.

The House That Isn't Mine

The house that isn't mine
lies five minutes from the Annisquam Bridge.
Old jazz standards play on the radio,
your mother has blue china.
We drink tea from her English pot.
In this house
there is nothing less
than politeness.

Which seems impossible
as I watch you on the green porch,
sipping a cold drink, ribena,
in remembrance of the Caribbean days.
But how can I know anything
when you are kissing
the backs of my knees?

There is a hole in the Annisquam Bridge.
The cars have to take an alternate route.
You can see straight down,
it's clear to the bottom of the river.
Broken pieces of white shell,
moss and rock
chill under the cold currents.

It's not the whistling fir trees
that trick me to sleep,
it's the hole in the Annisquam Bridge
widening under my heart.

Horrible Tangents

While clearing the land, Walter
accidentally chops down her favorite
apple tree. She is in the cabin
feeding the dog, which he forgot
at the lumber yard earlier that morning.
She is still not speaking to him.
He walks toward the cabin,
determined to tell her the truth.
In the cabin, she remembers
how awful being separated from Walter
was, almost as awful as living with
him now.

It's easy to say you don't want children
until you think about not having them.

She doesn't know why, but
it makes her sad to think of eating
watermelon with Walter.

Abilene

In another time
I am in Welfleet with my father.
I am too young to understand that life
is a gift he gave me. On the beach it is dark.
Frightened, I reach for his hand.
He tells me a joke about Texas. He hates Abilene.

Years later in an orange hotel room in Abilene,
I know how traveling kills time,
and why strangers touching hands
would appeal to you. Father,
you are still a child, afraid of the dark.
What has become of your life?

As a boy, your photograph appeared in *Life*.
"The most beautiful boy in Abilene."
In your white summer suit, your eyes looked especially dark,
like your mother's and mine. After all this time,
you still cannot forgive her, or your father
for not speaking as she hit your face and body with her hands.

I always fall in love with men who are left-handed.
The same thing ruined my mother's life.
You didn't drink, unlike her father,
and you were determined to leave Abilene.
To please her, you began to pray for the first time.
But loneliness is as bright as a lighthouse in the dark.

■ ■ ■

The sound of the ocean in the pitch dark
is like the whisper of lovers touching hands.
I never used to think about misplacing time,
or the possibility of carrying a life
inside me. There is no ocean in Abilene.
I am one year younger than you were when you became my father.

Sometimes I think I may never find a father
for the child I want to bring out of the darkness.
There are painful secrets in Abilene
that were handed down to you and you have handed
them to me. There is sadness on the edges of my life.
Nothing will free me from you except time.

One dark winter night in Abilene,
my father was reading *The New York Times*
when suddenly, he took life by the hand.

ROBERT MCDOWELL

Into a Cordless Phone

On Reelection Night the news was bad.
He called his oldest friend. They talked for hours,
Cursing groundhogs chewing up the line,
Transcontinental gobblers. His friend was trying
Out a cordless phone.
                                  "I'm moving now,"
He said, pushing through the back screen door.

"I cut my grass early this afternoon.
It looks just like the flattop cut you wore
In school. Suzy loved to skate her palm
Across your varsity plateau until
You graduated to the shaggy look.
I'm not the one who got invited to
Her parents' cabin at Lake Arrowhead!
Her family OK'd only right-wing nerds
Like Eddie Planck and Nehemiah Boone.
So tell me who you voted for. You won't?
Go walk along an unemployment line
And see how they take the news. You've done it? Where!"

He didn't catch the response of the unemployed
Because the corded voice had broken up.
I have no line, he thought, and glanced at stars
As if an operator might appear.
Instead a shooting star arced east to west
And something to his inner ear said *Walk*.
So heading west he crossed his neighbor's yard.
He stopped to stroke a basset hound, then dialed
His cordless phone and said hello. A sound
Washed over static, buried it in verbs—

"Run! Pack! Get your things and go!"
The dog he was scratching yelped and shook its head.
The crash of something falling shot from the house.
"Hello!" he said to the phone. "Hello! Hello!"
A wave of static rolled in to answer him.

He hurried past the house and crossed the street
To Earhart Park. By the lake the phone was silent.
Only laughter from a grove off to his right
Came in to him. He heard a bottle break
And hurried on until he faced her statue.
Staring up at the missing aviatrix
He raised his phone and spoke. "Come in," he said,
"For God's sake tell me where you are tonight."
The statue stared as if he didn't exist,
And nothing on his phone disputed it.
Farther down the path he chose a spot
To lean against a pole and warm his face
In yellow light that made the stars go out.
He thought of spy planes grazing the bleak Pacific;
He thought of rumors never verified
And wandered into the Children's Area
Where he sat on a swing and dialed his boyhood home.
Was it his mother he was speaking to?
He talked and talked about a day in school,
Then caught himself, fearing local news:

MAN ON SWING CALLS HOME ON CORDLESS PHONE

His cordless phone was dead, his mother, too.
Amelia hadn't answered. No one spoke.

He left the park and crossed Elm Avenue,
Then circled round the Billings' swimming pool.
Maybe water cleared its frequency,
Because his phone was rafting one low voice:

"You can't sit out there every night," it said.
"Nothing you can do will bring him back."
Another voice was sobbing while it spoke,
As soft as water lapping in the pool.
Then crying leveled off in a woman's voice:
"I just ran in to get the phone," she said.
"He was sitting in his playpen in the sun."
Her voice collapsed as he pushed through a gate.

The smell of garbage billowed out of cans.
His phone was mad with voices changing every
Twenty steps or so: *Sausage and anchovies—*
Feed the dog or shoot it! I don't care!—
I told you never play with Daddy's eyes!—
Take this, please, and try to get some sleep.—

He thought he should hang up but couldn't bring
Himself to disconnect his neighborhood.
He ducked a squad car, crouching behind a hedge,
And tried to eavesdrop on their radio.
He dialed 911 and said *Police*;
Another voice screamed *Fire* and he ran.
Crossing a familiar lawn he hopped a fence,
Then crept up to a door and dialed his phone.
"Hello," he whispered, "can you hear me now?"
His daughter's southern drawl was sweet with sleep.
"Go call your mother to the phone," he said.
His wife came on. She said his voice was odd,
"Like someone's sitting in a well," she said.
His friend's long-distance, earnest voice broke in
But faded after shouting the word *Where*.
He said to his wife "I will not sleep tonight,"
But he dropped the phone on the lawn and went inside.

The Backward Strut

When his telephone rings at 3 A.M.
And nobody hangs up and nobody speaks,
It comes to him that childhood
Is so remote it belongs to someone else.
Later, dozing in his favorite chair,
He dreams he can leap into moonlight
And be only vaguely aware
Of children, rebuked, taunting parents,
Of the alley crunching and gobbling, claiming its own.

Awake he sits at table and stares at the phone,
Hoping she'll unlock her language box.
He wonders what the dog knows, lying in a heap,
And the cat whose drug is an open window.
Maybe they'd like to listen to the radio,
But there's too much heartache on the air.
He feels like a man who opens a closet
To find another's clothes hanging inside.

Is he destined to live out his life
A lowercase letter among capitals?
Is he the test chemical that never pans out?
He remembers how at his christening he wiggled,
Evading the holy spray of water.
He thinks how there is no song to fit this life,
How the lyric is just like a wishbone—
A rush from the heart, a crack, and that's that.

The Usual Immigrant Uncle Poem

He feared money so much he was known
to shake and sweat in line at the register.

Once, they say, he broke down and wept.
And it seemed funny to us at Christmas

when he wore
his sister-in-law's underwear

on his head.
But we did not know

how it had been
back in Pereyaslav

or whatever other place
I never saw, and so

can't care for, really,
where they took his father,

a famous judge and orator,
and stood him against the wall

and so on.
Still, that doesn't quite explain the money.

The Sunday Before Easter

Dreadful it is
how here and there
endlessly God disperses
whatever lives.
                    —Hölderlin

I

I prayed each twilight with the crickets
as a boy to another boy, rapt
in his mother's blue-gowned arms:

Otche Nash.

Concentration is prayer;
poetry the private psalm.

Sunday before Easter,
before dawn revives
the city with its debonair
starlings, startled by weather

to wooing, behind
my desk, from where
in the window I can see your double
I pray the only way I can.

I tell you my stories
because they are mysteries,

II

because
the little god who dwells within,
reflecting God, creating
worlds with names, remembers.

My country, formerly the sun,
became the oil-slicked water;

sapped pine barrens and barren
suburbia;

the "Venice of New Jersey"
since it flooded every year;

at times mountains
and ignitable, polluted air

feel familiar
as the silk of your bed,

the blue-gold silk of your breasts.

III

Lviv, Peremyshl, Berchtesgaden:
there God flared in
his latest conflagration, disguised
or agonized
green;

booted, buckled,
moustache trim, chin
shaved clean as an apple,

■ ■ ■

proud of himself,
his shining discipline,
the moral courage to shelve
tobacco, moonlight, women.

He puffed himself especially
on his talent for division,
like that evolutionary
wonder, the amoeba;

for rising early, spitting
in his own glum sun,
showering in splinters
of ice-water without wincing,

marching in unison
with himself, raising legs
muscled as if modeled by Rodin.

And he was proud
of his spired libraries
outstripping Alexandria

where the dead speak and the living are silent.

He often visited museums
ransomed by lions,
accompanied by an interpreter
from the far city of Babel.

God torched houses.
He castrated boys, inspired
women burning for food
to murder their husbands.

■ ■ ■

He turned his people back to light.

I saw none of this.
But I remember.

IV

I remember and rehearse it
for you, whose perfect breasts
still cannot balance
the scales of justice.

These fairy tales mother
lent me for lullabies.
What once delivered me to sleep
now keeps me up

long after the emaciated hands
of the clock unclasp
and splay to quarter-cross
and the cat, and you, snore.

I tell you because
I come from a country
which no longer exists

and my name will not give me away.

V

Because it happens again
at a different address:
the Lord himself lashes
himself.

The Voyagers

for Sven Birkerts

The bottom of the sea is cruel.
　　　　　　—Hart Crane

1

Each week they meet to rehearse
The Losing of the Teeth.

On the boat coming over
he brooded the apotropaic water.

Sea of Withdrawls.
Sea of Deep Breathing.

Body, suffer
a sea change.

When his dentures
dropped out,

his wife screamed:
"Part of a man

overboard!"
The sailors spat and ignored her.

2

He survived.
They arrived. Settled. Smiled shyly.

Made their way.
Into the ghetto.

Out to the suburbs.
Children, money, sunflowers.

But what he knew
he kept to himself.

Gaping nightly
at the half-empty glass,

fingering his jaw
(a fair fit).

That no man willingly ever
gave up his teeth.

CAROL MOLDAW

The Watercolor

for Sharon

The thinnest most adventurous
strokes trail the hills and cross
the horizon, cross the hand-drawn
blurry border and (they are trees)

seem to sway, abandoning
the cultivated landscape
to lean over the uncropped
outskirts of the page.

Two trees pierce the horizon.
A field lighter, greener,
than the orange-yellow hills
a stream divides with the same

wintry blue as the white sky.
One of the three flowers
is you say a heart and who's
to disagree—it's yours and visibly

suggestive, even to the blackness
at its core. A heart enough like
any other, a flower in a field, a spot
of blackness deepening the red.

Not extraordinary that strokes
are trees, but these are
yours, of the same ink and hand
as the stream's bank, the hill's

■ ■ ■

ridge, the border trees trespass,
and the flower like a heart
I keep coming back to because
at the black center it bursts.

The Crossroads

for Julie

One moonless night I bring three yarrow stalks,
an obsidian disk, herbs, to the straight-backed chair,
poised, and topaz-eyed, like a red fox,

for auguries, angry skirrings in the air,
the gravel path up-scuffed, a streetlight blown.
But what clarifies in a candle's sudden flare,

a long thin nose and pointy chin, is my own
three-quarter silhouette, dispersed
head-on, the way water's shattered by a stone.

Once I would have turned away, and cursed,
sulking like that scrawny black cat I gave
milk to last spring, who had me woo her first.

But now it's my Mother's long black cloak I'd have,
her glistening skullcap of stars, her brindled pack,
as I stalk the earth, rounding it like a wave.

Midnight. No moon loops the zodiac.
Drugged, she sleeps dreamless in a dark cave,
one kitchen match to light her way back.

Jude:

My frenzies you call wildflowers.

A bridge and a stream
emboss the wide-brimmed China vase
where you arrange them.

Transmarine

An open hull nudging reeds and sand,
she kept to herself the pleasure he provoked,
the undercurrent dimpling as he stroked,
and drifted, slackly moored under his hand.
Turning to him, she let him loose the knot,
drop the rope, and push his foot against
the pier to lift her free. Her muscles tensed;
he took her like a sail the wind had caught
and guided her until she guided him,
and when they were no place that either knew,
where sky and sea and shadow echoed blue,
they plunged—and were knocked back at the world's rim.

KAREN MURAI

Florida

I have this nightmare someone dresses me
in a mermaid suit and makes me work for a
living, and I blame it on Florida,
a state that makes its way through my dreams
like a rubber shark. Florida,
state of biggest intentions,
new state of swelldom, inviting us all
to jump through the window.
And then I'm dressed in pink
at a flea market where recent retirees
sell the memories they're tired of
and machine guns sit on cardboard tables
surprising us with quiet before turning
into movie stars. This is where
good ole boys fizz like a swamp,
try on hats to keep their tender brains
from swelling, and only the alligators
show any wisdom, shrinking from heat
to taste primeval mud. And then
the cities start singing, the cities
that look strangely new, as if the
sky rained cosmetics or the fountain of youth
were real—but only for steel.
And their midnights swivel inside a glass,
and their mornings cough up flags,
and the calories are in the worries
as finely tuned as submarines.
The Cubans win blondes and walk away
with the show and I have to drink
just to stay even. I have to balance
between maudlin and macabre like a
good TV script. And I have to remember
that this is all in style,
the way America is in style again—
big, smiling, and recently laundered.

Sitting on Zero

All winter I have been waiting
for luck to show its new tooth,
writing a letter to something I can't
address, moving faster than iridescence.

And certain glances caught in my hair.
I thought of America in the 50's,
a landscape of lacquered suburbia,
and so many plaster stableboys

holding back darkness with their
little lamps. Such brittle hope.
It takes the air out of my lingo
and fills the heart with boxes. I

sit as tuned as a pair of white gloves,
but the silence gets all the oxygen,
and it doesn't seem fair to have
so many empty minutes knitted

over my head. What's needed is
combustion, a little friction in thought,
static attraction, the way a taxi
sticks to rain in my mind,

the sound of a slap in the dark,
and the crazy balance of a
promise. What's needed is the speech
that takes a kite, but it all seems

■ ■ ■

so distant, evanescent, as far away
as flutes, and I have found the art
in waiting, ironing shirt after shirt,
while the pool in my ear fills with stones.

It is not enough, this. It is not
ever enough. But what havoc can be
packed in a kiss will find its way to me,
scratching the door, an animal home.

A Small Demand

We want our fevers
when we want them.
Girls with new haircuts
still buzzing at the neck.
Boys collared with infection
catching kisses in a
rearview mirror. A
little deception
is always a little nice,
a little hand
calling from a curtain.
Patience mimics age
and is something to be cut
like an umbilical
to leave us
swaying like gospel.
Put your feet on the table.
Watch how hands become
shadow and shadow a
demand. Now. Here.
Over the phone.
Roll out the piano
with the girl slung over.
Let me tell you a movie
only make it silent.
Just a lamp, a muzzle,
and a slow dissection.

Declaration of Independence, II

And yet, one hates to change.   Ten years of intimacy!
The humility of admitting one has made mistakes.
Ten springs down the drain and the sodden aches
of ten maple-dunned autumns.   Crisp snows into April
which made us step back.   Not far enough!   Thank God for Brooklyn.
Though, ideally, life shouldn't be a declaration of anything,
but gentler, kinder, sweeter, more like home.

To which busy men resorted in the afternoons
after long lunches.   They pulled up their silk socks
and were gone.   One needs, of course, ideas and theories.
But this poem's the cement I am so grateful for.
No more discontinuity!   Effusiveness
is often deafness.   Not sparing a glance for in.

And not the nineteenth century.   Anachronisms
are a form of ostrichism.   Exile!
That way sprains the ankle.   As in rhythms,
a fourth-grade class.   I'd rather be lame
it seems, than hoof, hoof, hoof it to the tune
of ladies, ladies.   Yes, if the mind's a snail,
then home begins in the imagination.

Omit nothing!   Her favorite punctuation mark
was the ellipsis.   Or the parenthesis.   Both monuments
to the aesthetic of hare.   Is to hop to hope?
Oh dear,   I'm up on my high horse again.   I know I'm afraid.
But of what?   Love's criminality?   Silence.
But not the kind when the day holds its breath, then rain.

She thinks too much.   Such women are dangerous.
To a tyrant maybe.   He, however, liking   (this
was another theory) hierarchies said: *I am afraid*
you will go crazy with all this poetry.   Hiss!
No.   More sane.   Separate church and state.
Thought is democratic.   *True.   And holy.*   Hmph!   Let cranes fuss
in their shrill arguments with obtuse pygmies.

Och!   the scrutiny of your nineteenth century chagrin!
Too late, I'm afraid.   I've been bluff for too long,
deaf to the gruff waves breaking at my iced feet.
I am no pelican.   I will not jettison
my mother and father for you, nor the whole world either.
But—love is not love if it's not dangerous.

True.   But some dangers are imaginary, a waste.
I'm sick of deaths and the insatiable spade.
The way Odysseus must have felt clinging to the rock
Charybdis tore him from.   He lost the flesh
of his fingers.   There's something pink in shock.
Pink cheeks, a gentlewoman fainting.   But my life isn't a book.
It hurts too much.   I'm buried now in ash.

In this way they carried on: To come home
or back to life . . .   I haven't the courage, I guess.
There is something to the business of love as a haven,
wet by no rains, pelted by no hail,
flogged by no wind.   Danger, yes, but not
suicide.   Nothing to be ashamed of in surviving.

Genitalia are the pinkest part of the body.
Oh, shut up.   Then there's generation.   Cranes.   No storks.
He fumed.   She wanted to be alone.   *Quirks!*
Whims!   And what do you call 'em.   Intuition.
It makes me sick.   But not to ditch him.   *An infatuation!*
You're stupefied by someone or other.   That's shoddy.
But true.   All right then, yes.   God's creation.

Odysseus permitted himself to be confiscated in mist
and led home by a chit of a girl.   Humility!
But anagke makes us do all sorts of things,
like hurrying home to Penelope, even if
it means dying in the process, giving up fame
or notoriety, abandoning one's name, becoming nobody.

A shit of a girl?   *Oh Lord, oh honestly.*
To sink to such depths.   No, what you say is true
and great.   But he didn't die, the hero of the *Odyssey*,
dragged home by the ear, seduced
by the ear.   That is all I'm trying to say.
Words . . . Words . . . Words.   For the sake of poetry,
don't accuse me of . . .   *Poultry?   Poultry?*

the old woman who looked like a chicken shrieked
a month later.   I'd left.   Saratoga Springs!
Used books.   Her daughter had just died.
And in the same breath, *have you heard Rock Hudson's gay?*
Absence, absence.   Absence and desire.
But I have some friends who are gay.   Not too lonely.

Mebbe you'd like this . . . Letters of Louisa May Alcott.
Confused, I nodded.   At home . . . horse-races!   *All life*
should be a vacation, he said bitterly.   I perused
the introduction: *The young women of today, wearing waterproofs,*
and India rubber boots, skating, driving,
and bicycling—in constant states of velocity
as well as emotion . . . that was 1888.
Och!   Abstractions keep us all from being lonely.
It was the love of islands which engaged us.
True intimacy is a kind of formality, someone sighed.
But we were afraid to run before the wind
and only came about instead of jibing,
afraid to find love's shakey equilibrium.

Penelope sets up house with Odysseus

Aetherials have no sex, said Fielding,
or wrote, anyway.   She'd read it that morning, mourning.
Later, they gathered the stiff bamboo, their arms heavy
with it, scissors wet with green filaments.
The pneumatic drill next door was hushed, on vacation,
as they came home and swished their fragment of nature
into the diminutive house, two-storied.   A bird-cage
for the humming bird.   Aetherials . . . but the diminutive house
had given her a wafer-thin body she could heft
on wings.   A triste touriste, she joked.   It wasn't true.
A happy tourist.   And was her felicity
unforgivable?   Something stupid in joy?   Was misery
more real—no! more true?   No!   There must be leavening in the bread
or the yeasty spirit dies.   Here happiness is blest.

BRENDA MARIE OSBEY

An excerpt from
Desperate Circumstance, Dangerous Woman

First you see the vision. Then you see
the woman who made you see.

MEMORY
1.
i sit in the front parlor
the window open from the floor
the hard rain rushing in
stinging like fire-ants
against my feet
the little cloth navy pumps mama had given me
set to one side
placed out of the wet.
do you know what hunger is?

i sit with the water
moving about my feet
remembering what it feels like to be touched:
my mother's hands parting my oiled hair
down the center
across the front;
my mother's hands bearing down on my back
rolling a little from place to place
as if
there were some secret place she could touch me
to help me cry
and just be done with it;
hands of some hoodoo-woman
cradling my face
bathing me in bamba and sweet basil
feeling with her fine wet hands
along my skull
along my spine;

the hands of lovers who thought they knew
something of desire—
good men some of them
with no way of knowing
how their own hands would betray them;
you percy
down on your knees on the hardwood floor
arms wrapped about me
groping with your palms and fingers
along my hips
my thighs:
please woman please
that's what you said
each time you bit my brown flesh
sucking up the little traces of blood
between clenched teeth.
did i cry?
did i cry?
no.
it was you kept saying
you got your hands on me woman
god-have-mercy you got your hands on me
but you stayed
didn't you?

you stayed the night.
you stayed all day the next day.
and when you came back the night after that
you said you couldn't come again.
you'd go home to your wife,
do all a man could,
give me anything—
if i'd just take my hands off you.
i remember your eyes, percy.
i don't know how to beg
that's how you said it
i don't know how to beg
but please

woman please
you got your hands on me and i just can't live like this

you walked out of the house
and across the porch.
you broke off a little stem of geranium in the corner.
i saw you press it tight between your fingers.
they smell of iron i said to you then.
always smelled of iron to me
like blood percy
like blood

i walked over
to where you crouched above the flowering clay pots.
i put one hand into your near-kinky hair.
percy i said
percy
don't you know what hunger is?

2.
the day we buried mama hangs in my mind
like a yellow cotton summer dress
on the clothesline out back.
what i remember?
how her sisters,
the two who outlived her,
argued with me over everything:
the plain wood coffin,
her body,
the clothes i chose to lay her out in,
the ribbon of blue silk
wrapped loosely about her folded hands
which held no meaning for them,
the mexican earrings hanging from her ears,
the mass of grey hair i would not let the mortician dye,
the nails shaped and painted
that moony opal color she wore so often,

and at the wake
the shameless way i touched her
holding feeling
her hands and face
kissing her eyes and mouth
as though she were a lover
or alive.

that night you lay against me
your face pressed deep
against the pit of my arm.
i rubbed your smooth neck with one hand.
you kissed my breast.
i thought of mama,
the yellow cotton dress
blowing
hanging
on the clothesline.

3.
ms. regina stands above me
above
my naked body laid out on the pile of burlap
filled with pungent roots
bruised herbs.
she steps around me in her stocking-feet
sprinkling scented waters
about the burlap
and my skin.
through the long window panes leading up from the floor
i can see
the slates on the rooftops
take on the faint light of a late sun going down.
ms. regina bends and puts both hands
into the earthen vessel beside my head.
she brings out the red cloth
and puts it to my body

begins to rub slowly
with a back and forth motion
my chest
my breasts
my sides
the soft of my belly
working her way
along the stretch of my body
singing in the same
sing-song voice she uses
for everyday speech.
i go back and forth
between a hard shaking chill
and the calm of yellow cotton dresses.
when ms. regina leaves me
i am thrashing almost to death.
when i wake the next morning
to the smell of thick coffee
and biscuits heavy with butter,
the shades are drawn.
i lie in bed beneath blue cotton sheets and comforters.
white towels and a wash basin await me
left in plain view
the way a woman ms. regina's age
would remember to place them.
i wash.
i peer into the looking-glass
tilted back against the window ledge.
when i let up the shade to see
there is ms. regina
in the backyard
hanging out the wash.

Alberta (Factory Poem/Variation 2)

1.
when my grandmother alberta was a girl
she worked in solomon's factory
alongside women
who stood to stitch men's suits
to hang from the shoulders of white mannequins
who would not say *thank you*
for the any number of needles sewn through flesh
to put food on the table
to keep children in school
or a husband home
to avoid the indignity of government "Relief"
to protect a mother or father
from the old folks' home.

my grandmother alberta was a girl when she first saw
women eating small sandwiches
or bread dry-long-so
from the hip pockets of their dresses
as they stood sewing
because they were given no time for lunch.
women bleeding through triple-layered toweling
afraid to leave their machines the length of time it took
to wash and change the wadded cloth between their legs
afraid to lose the pay
solomon's sons doled out at week's end.
and more than once
a woman who had to go—
but not soon enough.
a woman sprawled against the white commode
the dark fluid slipping across the floor
and the two or three other women

standing guard against the door
hiding away the solution:
quinine and castor oil
to bring on the quick violent abortion
that might let you stagger back to a machine
to stand and stitch together
collars and lapels
welt pockets to decorate white mannequins
propped up in better stores
throughout the southern region.

she was a woman with a husband and children
by the time she knelt
between her own baby-sister's knees
and caught the nearly full-term moving mass
felt its warm head in her hand
before she flushed it down the toilet
and wiped between galena's legs.
all kinds of things i saw and did she said
working in a factory of women
and it was no time
before she was promoted to floor-walker
freed from the stooping posture
of those women who stitched
heads down in silence
or singing across to one another
lyrics spun out above the hum of motors and needles.
often it was the threadcutters
whose bottoms bore into the long wooden benches
where they squatted gap-kneed more than sat
who tossed out a line
and it would come back
stretched by the heavier voice
of some woman who stood all day
wiping the oil from her fingers
into the blackened wood
of her upright atlas machine.
such a woman sent back a line stretched to endurance

altogether seamless
against the drone of motors
working at full pitch.

my grandmother alberta walked the boarded spaces between the women.
she walked.
she kept time.
is it any wonder she asks
as if i were to answer
is it any wonder
we sang like that?

2.
a great deal happened the year i was nine.
so i suppose i was nine the year my mother
not my grandmother
taught me to embroider.
i sat cross-legged on the hard floor
piercing my fingers
bunching up the coarse cloth
that would become dishcloths
tea cosies
for my grandmother
who surely had enough of one
and small use for the other.
later
much later
i learned to fashion
elaborately flowered pillowslips
dresser scarves
lace edgings she loved to store up
to show off to relatives
foolish enough to visit
during the long new orleans summers.
your mother does a fine stitch she says
watching me lift then re-set
the heavy iron over the face-down designs
as i was taught.

when i do not look up from my task
she offers at a lower register:
sewing is different.
no one teaches you to sew.

3.

the men who worked the mezzanine
the cutting floor above
looked down across the vast crowded floor of women,
rolled up white shirtsleeves,
took white chalk in hand,
marking and cutting.
men's labor.
calling for a certain daring precision.
and higher paying
affording short breaks
to smoke or eat
to drink rc cola on the stair landing
to take time to look across the floor of crowded women
on the ground level
manufacturing blues.

4.

"we stood together.
we worked together.
we cussed old man solomon
and the day he ever set foot inside this city.
we cursed the cloth we stitched together
and the lives it cost us to stitch it.
we cursed the babies we dropped
and the men who gave them to us,
the bodies, our own bodies,
that held to them in the womb,
the conditions that dogged us so
and made us drop them
by choice or by accident
by long standing in heat or cold,
the perfect solution handed over to us

by the women we stood among,
manufacturing blues
for all we were worth."

these are the last words
the words my grandmother
did *not* say to me.
my grandmother alberta is dead.
she can not speak to me further
of her youth among those women
her and her baby sister
down on the ground level
among their upright atlas machines.
she can no longer hold up at eye level
her slightly yellowed middle finger
sewn through the nail
the smooth even split
where the machine tore flesh and nail
and after all those years
the nail refused ever to grow together.
my grandmother alberta is dead and buried
and reduced to ash.
i am her last remaining evidence:
the smooth
straight
seam.

JACQUELINE OSHEROW

Looking for Angels in New York

All this travelling around and I've learned
Nothing less obvious than this: that each
Piece of the world has something missing.
Home again, I have forgotten the stops of the trains,
My friends' phone numbers. I haven't even the heart
To take the maps out, to say, "Here I have been,
Here and here." I want to explain that there
Can be no adequate descriptions, but you will think
I mean the differences are insurmountable,
When it is this vast sameness over everything
I cannot name, the thing you wait for
And do not believe in when it's come and gone,
The words that will not stand still
Long enough for you to take a picture.

My friend asks questions and I answer.
He says he read the Metropolitan Life
Building is based on something Italian.
I look at it and shrug, "Not that I know,"
And then I see the campanile of San Marco,
Squat, granite, white instead of red.
It will become my personal comfort
In the skyline, one of those public things
You have no right to but you say you own.

If Jacob had rested in New York, he
Would have seen angels on elevators,
And St. Mark, though an insurance salesman,
Would certainly have witnessed miracles.

■ ■ ■

I don't necessarily have to see
An angel, I just want to see some wings,
Even a flash of them, gliding, moving
Up and out, a balloon some child
Has let go of, smaller and smaller in
The sky, only wings, definite, white wings.

From the number seven train out to Queens,
A chance glimpse of the unisphere brings
The future in its purest form, the whole
World connected by picture telephones
And cars that look like earthbound rocketships.
Odd that they should have left the silver globe
Still standing there, now the children it was
Built for have all grown. The space between the
Continents seems eerie now, foreboding,
And the dazzling modern sculpture weirdly
Archaic, almost shocking, like the face
Of a great movie star no longer young.

Who would have thought that people would reject
The picture telephone, the moving sidewalk,
That I would come home from all my travels
To New Jersey, to settle for a bit
Of quiet and some green, and the moment
On the hill before the Lincoln Tunnel
When I really do possess something extraordinary.
Loyal, I pick out my Metropolitan Life,
At night drenched in a white light almost blue.
Who can know that by day it is not brick
And red and surrounded by a great piazza
Opening on water, that, in the huge
White space we cannot see, there is no thick
Flock of cooing pigeons, taking off, alighting,
In a constant, dreamy fluttering of wings.

The Yiddish Muses

I—unneeded, a poet among Jews—
Growing, like wild grass, from a soil not ours
In an alien world I sing of the cares
Of men in a desert beneath alien stars.
                    —Mani Leib (1883–1953)

They arrive, always, unexpected,
Silent as the glide of angels
On six wings. Only the idea of sound,
Wind that for a moment might be ocean.
I want to catch them, to make something
For them, a city or at least a psalm,
But I have nothing to build it with.
Yiddish is no language for poetry, so homely
On the page, vowels instead of silences.

Unneeded, a poet among Jews,
I end up wandering the streets
With unknown visitors, who speak
In a language round and thick
As pillows squashed against my head.
They are telling dreams, so old,
So corny, dreamed by now in almost
Every language and a few elements:
Wood, stone, even gold, preserved
In cloth with needles and silk thread.

They have left a little dreaming
Everywhere: watery cities, towered cities,
Even in Cordoba, blank with sun, so white
And so unlikely, they left a whole room

Engraved with psalms. Judah Halevi
Left a palace and a family. Tired
Of poetry and dreams, he headed East.
After that, no one is certain.
They say he was trampled by a Turkish horse
As he kissed the earth, arriving in Jerusalem.

You will tell me this is not a pleasant story,
But you know nothing about dreams.
What would have happened if the sun
Had bowed to Joseph? I know for a fact
It would have killed him and any unsuspecting
Bystanders. I suppose we must be patient
Here, at the stony end of the ladder.
Only angels can go up and come back down.

I stay awake nights, though I'd give
Anything to see the curved backs
Of stars, and wonder who needs ladders
With three sets of wings. I watch shadows,
Cast by my Venetian blinds, stretch
Across the ceiling like the tracks
For unknown trains. Can you blame me
If I ride and ride, unneeded as I am
And dangerous, a dreamer among Jews.

The muses burst out laughing, "Some dream."
All morning, in synogogue, they chuckle
As they praise The Name, "Some prize to be a traveller
Among Jews." Still, they manage silence
For the eighteen prayers, establishing that routine
Miracle, reordering of heavens, Jerusalem
Rising like the sun above their heads,
Above, even, the women's section, higher
Than any memory its walls and domes.

Sonnet

after Lorenzetti's Deposition from the Cross

He is like a cloud that for an instant
Shaped a man, but has begun to spread,
To stretch the limbs, the torso, twist the head
So that it falls, upside-down, against
His mother's, her forehead to his cheek,
Her eye against his closed eye. And his thick
Gold hair filters through her hands like sand.
One saint bends to kiss a foot, one a hand,
One holds him just beneath the falling arm
And one more holds the thighs, presses his lips
Against the cloth that covers them and weeps.
What is the Resurrection to them?
It will not stay those thighs, those arms, that hair,
This thin, white mist that soon will disappear.

DONALD REVELL

Central Park South

The way the buildings curve (as if a thought
or big dream you could never really get
your brain to go about fixing for you, had
for once become a grand hotel, an all-
forgiving grey exterior like that
which faces north across the park and loves
you) makes you think of any afternoon
at five in late October and of how
the girl you followed used to disappear
into the Plaza. Nothing has changed along
that street. You walk. You watch a limousine
go by and look for actresses. The light
is still what you remember having thought of
when you thought of Venice, Henry James,
or being happy—blue, with a touch of grey
and orange. Only your nerves can rot; the rest
goes on discriminating, particularly
places. There have always been those places,
real corners that can stay there and forgive your
wanting a drink or having once believed
that love should be conducted openly
and in the daytime. If you could wrap your mind
around the park, the way these walls do, you
would rot a little more slowly. Maybe if
you dreamed the way a building dreams you
might even heal. Remembering that girl
was not a bad way to start. Just follow her
along the park side now, but go west, away
from that hotel that always put an end
to everything. At Columbus, turn and head
for the museum where they put the bones
together; you will be glad of bones by then,
or with a bit of luck, be side by side
with the girl, having forgotten. But either way,

romantic Venice is alive in New York
again. The lights are as blue as ever; the park
is colorful at night, in October. What
you came for were the curves. You got them. Look
at how the buildings curve around and close
in lovingly. You had been following love
then. Now it is a street beside the park.

Fauviste

Five minutes with his paintings and I remember.
This is life on the boats, and any place
to stand is a dead wife bobbing under daubs
of wet lanterns, not a thought of home,
no imagining how the three beds
of iris will burst and stand beside the house.

Five minutes, and I cannot picture my own life.

I don't think there is any use looking backward.
The boats were lowered by other hands than mine
as I slept. When I awoke, we were already
far from the sinking and had new names.
My wife was dead or in love with someone else
in another boat. At night, we strung up lanterns
and we had five minutes of a beautiful painting.

We were never rescued. And I am sure
that rescue only happens to the faithful,
that seeing five minutes of the world with no wife
and all the lanterns hanging close to the water
changed my eyes into other things that see
but cannot see rescue when it comes.

I see my wife and flowers in everyone's hands.

I don't think there is any use painting irises.
The three beds that I know my wife tended
were lost at sea. Their petals washed towards land
and into the mouths of rivers painted by Frenchmen.
I cannot picture them. I only know that they fell to pieces
as I slept and that someone in France made something
out of them that is my life on the boats.

A Setting

in memory of John Cheever

There is nothing Orphic, nothing foreign.
The deep greens of a suburban June,
the lawns, the orientalia,
are enough, for now, to make you sing.

The deep greens of a suburban June
drift from oriel to oriel and
are enough, for now, to make you sing
into the dark you've watched

drift from oriel to oriel. And
now the air around the porchlights curves
into the dark you've watched,
changing into the colored air of romance.

Now the air around the porchlights curves
like hours in summer, like desire,
changing into the colored air of romance
your first home breathed into you.

Like hours in summer, like desire,
what you cried out each June
your first home breathed into you,
became the best of you.

What you cried out each June—
"There is nothing Orphic, nothing foreign!"—
became the best of you,
the lawns, the orientalia.

Emily Dickinson's Mirror, Amherst

Its flecked surface a map of disappearing islands,
the glass imposes a narrowing, flat sense
of time and limited space upon the room
at all angles. Looking into it head on,
I feel contained and ready to understand
the short lines' skewed New England syntax mouthed
into so strict a frame. A discipline
of words arrayed for the bridal and no groom
wanted. In each of us, there must be one
oracular, strait emptiness a hand's
breadth across that is ourselves in proud
fear, looking into our own eyes for doctrine
and the one audience whose accents we can
share wholly. The purist's God. Pride's mirror and island.

Elegies for Etsuko

I.

Begin with the last and unrecorded scene—
how rashly, with a length of rope,
she'd gathered up an end to hope?
Or unravel these six years
to where my life first tangled up with hers?
Or, midway, to that greater knot: again

the line of thought loops back, heart-
broken, to where she reckoned life to start.
Her wedding day. The Bride.
And in truth, that day I shed
a veil of happy tears: to see that snow
mountain of kimono,

and falling from the pinnacle
of her lacquered wig, the fog of silk
over a face too shy, too proud
to raise. Who'd made her up?—the natural
milk of her skin absorbed in chalk,
a slope of powder

down to her collar, pulled low at the back.
Viewed from behind, a woman's neck
is (say the Japanese—and so she'd say)
her most erotic feature.
But I think she was that day
a hybrid sort of fantasy, a creature

■ ■ ■

sparked by a wand, then shrinking like that star
when the TV goes black. Am I unkind?
Darling, we guess at how you came unwound;
at how many times you drunkenly replayed
that trade of sacred *sake* and were made
Queen for a Day again on the VCR.

II.
Given how brief a spell
happiness usually is, and the ways
people are forever failing us,
with time it shocks me less you didn't mind
leaving the two of them behind;
yes yes, I see that, I see it very well . . .
But do you mean to say you were willing
never again to wear a new dress?
And never again to choose one for your daughter?
Long before she was born, or mine was,
we'd go on window-shopping sprees
in children's stores. Saccharine, but true.
I can't stand it, one of us would say; *can you?*
—A bonnet or a tasseled sock would send
us off: half-stifled, giggling cries . . .

In the end, you didn't think to find
even a rag to shield her eyes.
Because you had gone blind.

III.
In Keiko's brain these words are Japanese
in bits and pieces   none of them is written
nobody's here to hear the words she knows
nobody's here   just mother on the ceiling
her face is closed her face   long face her hair
not crying now   she tries *okaasan*   mother
the word that calls up everything
and nothing moves at all   oh there's her ball

IV.

Ages between the day I left Japan
and the first time I saw you again: the last
time, too. New Year's Eve in Rome.
Foreigners both, we soon pick up that word-
less, winking giddiness we'd had: as light
a burden as our daughters, whom we lift
to watch the soaring fireworks. Each time the sky
blows up again, and then begins to cry
in sputters—whistling, molten streaks of tears—
we laugh: *See? Nothing to be afraid of* . . .
And in the window, too, we see ourselves
reflected kindly in our girls: *They'll learn
to be mothers just like us.* How long since you
were known as Hara-san (Miss Hara)! These days
it haunts me, that when you married you erased
your first name too—and as an honor asked
I call you by a childhood nickname, Ekko.
Ekko. Echo. *Ecco*: the champagne
cork pops, the skies explode, repeat
that automatic gunfire to the heart:
Ekko, you would not toast the year again.

V.

These vacant months I've tried to disavow
that something's happened to you, something dire.
I know you're gone for good. And this is how

I've figured out you've made your final bow
(at last, the proof's so small that we require!)—
were you alive, you would have called by now.

More clues come than I'd willingly allow:
if they hadn't shoveled you into the fire
(I know you're gone for good, and this is how)

■ ■ ■

and buried you beneath a maple bough,
you would have dropped a line or sent a wire.
Were you alive, you would have called by now.

The phone's the lifeline of the lost *hausfrau.*
But now what's at your ear? The angel's lyre?
I know you're gone for good, and this is how

I turn the same line over like a plow,
since there is nothing further to inquire.
Were you alive, you would have called by now

to greet me in your faulty English grammar.
Your silence shows precisely how you are.
I know you're gone for good. And this is how:
were you alive, you would have called by now.

VI.
Up here's where you end up. Room with a view
in (of all places) Edinburgh, though who's
willing to predict she'll feel at home
with dying anywhere? Why not the random
furnished flat in Scotland? What we own,
what we are owned by, are no less transient
than other plots of earth we briefly rent . . .

Parking across the street, we stay inside
as if we hope (we fear) you're still up there
in a state of mind precarious but alive:
you mustn't be allowed to think we're spying.
You seem to know I knew I'd have to come;
that your husband's brought me here, a half-year later.
Oh, anything we do may set the chain

■ ■ ■

reaction going once more in that brown
study of your brain; we'd have to live
through losing you again; we'd have to choose . . .
Why is it your apartment's set ablaze
and no one else's? Why is it in the pitch
of six o'clock in winter, nothing's on
in all the building—just the silhouette

of a woman coming slowly to your window
to watch the Christmas lights down Princes Street
illuminate toy people and their things?
. . . Unless, somehow, you're giving us the ghost
of a chance to guess how singularly bright
you'd felt yourself to burn, engulfed in flame
none of us ever saw, much less put out?

VII.
Once, in Kyoto, we gossipped past the temple
graveyard where you'd lie, on to the shrine

where you wanted us to buy two paper dolls:
featureless, pure white, the kind a child

cuts in hand-holding chains across a fold.
An old priest had us sign them both for luck.

I wrote across the heart, you down the spine,
then quaintly (so I thought) you drew two smiles . . .

That was before you snapped your pretty neck.
Happy you may have been, but never simple.

VIII.
Happy you may have been . . .
There were whole years when I'd have said
you were happier than anyone.
You've now been dead

(and been enclosed
in the double mystery of what
that is, and why you thought
it might be best)

for long enough it's time
to more than forgive the sin
of express despair, the crime
of not being what we seem,

or of not being anything
in particular . . . for isn't that
really what you feared you were?
Sometimes the note

you didn't write (because
you needed all the energy you had
to do the deed? because
there's no cause in the mad,

for whom the world's a small
footstool kicked aside?)
looms real and legible.
It says you died

because you'd come to think that love
is not enough. Well, I'd
probably have agreed,
advised you to find work, to read.

And now love's pain, your curse,
is all I have. Forgive me . . . What worse
punishment for suicide
than having died?

IX.

On the master list we keep
imagining the scribes still keep
religiously, up there in space,
of every human life, let
them not neglect to fill the line
for Etsuko Akai, who's gone
    from Earth at twenty-eight.

In the impossible blue dark,
let all the bearded saints and rain-
bowed angels sorrow can invent
take her, who never made her mark,
and gladly mark the day for love
not of what she might have been,
    but what she humbly was.

For surely they have reams of time
to celebrate the perfect moon
set in her attentive face,
where pallidly, one shallow crater—
a pockmark time could not efface—
glossed the ancient and unwritten
    flaws of her Creator.

Since they'll all be there for ages,
let them in their inventory
preserve in lucent, gilt-edged pages
those things I would myself record:
such as the way she'd tell a story—
she'd race, and trip, and laugh so hard
    we'd ask her to start over.

Made in the Tropics

Bobby Culture ("full of roots and culture")
and Ranking Joe ("Man Make You Widdle
Pon Your Toe") shift down
in the gloaming, snap off
their helmets, kill their engines, park
one thousand cubic centimeters
of steeled precision Japanese art.
Their bands drive up
in fur-trimmed vans, unload and unwrap
the hundred-watt speakers, thousand-watt amps,
mikes and mike stands,
guitars, cymbals, steel cans,
at the Blue Room Lawn on Gun Hill Road
by the Bronx Botanical Gardens.
The sun over Jersey
kicks and drops
into the next of its ready-made slots,
and, like a dark lotion
from a pitcher poured, night fills
the concrete hollows and the grass
cools in the projects,
the glowing lakes contract
around their artifical islands,
the gardens breathe
easier in the dwindling fever
of today's unbearable summer.
They say the tropics
are moving north,
the skull-cap of ice melting
from both the pole now pointed
toward the sun
and the one pointing away.
But what they say is hardly heard here,
where the cooling brickwork

engine-red Edwardian
railroad flats empty
of their tenants, who gather
in twos and threes, float down
from the stations
and congregate at the Blue Room Lawn
to celebrate Independence
Day in Jamaica.
The bass line fires up.
From Savanna-La-Mar to Gun Hill Road
the backwash of reggae spirals
to its perch, ripples
and flares its solar wings
along the upended moving limbs
as if a chain were passed through every wrist,
as if a chain were tied from hip to hip.
The sun does what it does because the earth tilts.

A Sketch from the Campaign in the North

Just before dawn the women are washing
skirts and blouses, slacks from Hong Kong
scrubbing their cotton on pock-marked boulders
cleaning their limbs with mud and lemons
along the turbid river.
At the edge of the jungle in surplus tents
the men are talking without weakness or strength
of the recent change in the government.
On the other bank the soldiers are waiting
for the sun to rise from the hills behind them
not smoking, not talking, in place and unmoving
as the leaves above them waver.
The day unfolds as if kept in a folder
on a desk in the capital.
The sun rises and blinds the river
the soldiers line up and fire from its cover
the air is gravid with sulfur
the river takes blood without changing color
a siren signals the end of the hour
and later in the capital
word is leaked to the foreign papers—
not even their souls climbed free to safety.
There are no handholds up that wall of light.

My Esmeralda

for S.O.K.

Some people like each other and are therefore like each other,
but I like you and therefore I'm
so original a burden on my time
that all the lifeguards ring their bells
when I rise from my exclusive underneath
to wash in your England of seaside hotels,

climb my perch and send off, over the panorama
of what's most yours—those glowing herds
of prehistoric bison, sunk in clear light
up to the eyes, browsing elsewhere
extinct skyhigh ferns—
my messenger birds,
speckled and superfine,
to soar the asymptotic line
that touches you at infinity. Big mama!

not once in any of the meretricious annals
I'm forced to read, have I read
of you, nor through the maps
I have to make sense of
have I ever watched you pass.
Among words, you're the meaning of "glass,"
and you as a river will cut your own channels.

This Fast-Paced, Brutal Thriller

There's always a killer with a name like Tony,
a tie-dyed shirt and a certain
sad history of deprivation:
just so much evil to get the plot going

down the edge of a formula
nickled and dimed
by years of repetition.
There's always an ocean near Hawaii or California

where the detective ponders the copy of a psalm
he once gave in commemoration
to his friend, the victim,
(they shared a tin hut in Vietnam)

over whose body the salt water swarms.
Something as strange and uncanny
as Taiwanese packing twine
has been wrapped around the legs and blue arms,

giving the detective, for his deduction, a sign
that the script changed tongues
in the middle of a scene,
and only he's left to render this line

to the bored, puzzled girl on whom the camera can't focus
because she stepped for a look
from another channel.
She stares right past him as she says, "Jesus,

■ ■ ■

this show, it's the pits."
And the faces start blending
on the molten screen:
screen before which the defeated imagination sits.

JASON SHINDER

From Magritte's Notebooks

I

I find myself alone in the middle of the night. I search the
house for no purpose and discover my mother is gone.
Noticing footprints on the steps and the pavement, I follow
these and come to the bridge over the Sambre, the local
river. My mother has thrown herself into the water. When
I fish out her corpse, her face is covered by her nightgown.
How proud, I felt, being the pitiful center of a tragedy.

II

The bell rings. It's my wife's lover. He introduces himself,
as we haven't met before. He is highly respectable, bour-
geois. I invite him in, step back to let him pass and, the
moment he sets foot in the drawing room, give him a tre-
mendous kick up the backside. He hesitates between the
multitude of reactions that come to mind. In the end he
sits down, as if nothing happened, on the chair, which I, as
if nothing happened, hasten to offer him.

III

One night I shared a room with a bird asleep in a cage. I
woke up and, by some glorious delusion, saw, instead of a
bird, an egg inside the cage.

IV

A little girl and I climb an old disused cemetery of a provin-
cial town. We explore the vaults whose heavy trap doors
we are able to lift. When we climb up again into daylight
the columns are broken and scattered among the dead
leaves.

V

Lying on the beach is a mermaid whose top half is that of a
fish and bottom half the belly and legs of a woman.

VI

In front of a window seen from inside a room I placed a picture representing exactly that part of the landscape which was covered by the picture. The tree in the picture representing the tree standing behind it, outside the room.

VII

A woman on a bicycle brushed past me, accompanied by a man, also on a bicycle. It was night, and I clearly saw the woman move away, her stockings white, and I was still very much aware of her even after she had disappeared around the corner.

VIII

The problem of the door is finding the opening. The problem of the rain is finding the great clouds which creep over the ground.

IX

I watched someone unroll a length of blue silk and the silk frightened me. I was afraid to come near it. Yet there was nothing threatening about it. The person showing it to me and smiling barely paid attention to it. At that moment, I became aware of where I was. We were on a Pacific Island, and there were women clinging to my sides, faces to the ground, not daring to look at this piece of silk they were seeing for the first time.

X

The first feeling I remember is when I was in a cradle, and the first thing I saw was a chest of drawers next to the cradle. The world presented itself in the guise of a chest.

Doppelgänger

At the end
of the highest balcony,
at the very edge
of the evening,
I step out to meet you.
I've seen you before:
on a hill
the color of wind,
on a beach
the color of bones.
Where have you been? you ask.
Nowhere. I haven't been anywhere.
I'm not even here, I say,
but I'm used to that.
You stand so close
I inhale your breath. I tell you
everything about my life
because you don't ask.
Maybe you're wearing gloves,
maybe a hat, maybe nothing.
Perhaps you ask:
What's kept you? Probably
you just stand there, pale
as the ghost the cold leaves
in my breath.
I lean over the balcony
above the ocean
and you pull at my sleeve
like a beggar
who wants something I don't have.
You might say
the moon is moving
the water closer.
You might not.

You turn your eyes toward me
like the dark chutes
of a double barrel shotgun.
I knew it would come to this,
I say, each of us threatening
to jump, but we don't.

The Living Mirror

After the storm,
the telephone poles, upright,
durable, add blue light to
blue light
along the snowy road.
The bay, with its brightening mirror,
slowly reflects
the silent clouds,
the faces that have carried me
to this town, etched
sixty miles into the cut glass
of the Atlantic.
The birds are lighter.
And the stones, drops of honey,
shine. How did they survive?
Two fisherman slip
into a trembling boat.
Again, they are face to face.
The sun flares up, rosy-pink,
clear, purple-edged.

[Ode]
To Marie Osmond

There you are again,
your crystal-perfect face
on the cover of the *Enquirer*.
It seems you're everywhere this Spring,
on more magazines than April has roses.
And yes, your series flopped, but you really are
more suited to the slit sequined dresses of NBC
than to *Family Circle* declarations of virginity.
Lips of a TV Venus should pucker, not pout.

And what a waste that the nine men you love,
hinted at in this week's *Star*, turn out
to be your father and eight brothers, that
the husband you dream of would be another
   perfect virgin.
Your daddy's Mormon domain is as barren
of life as his head is of hair; let *me* be your
   conquering
consort and you'll be a far richer heiress, when
the shadows of Utah's long Winter are fled,
and you stand alone on the Rockies, surveying
an ancient city of soft buildings, which
   transubstantiate
and interpenetrate in moon-aluminum evening,
   where warm
headlighted insects dance in circles, and golden
movie star men stand upright among beasts,
holding tokens of serpents, sunglasses,
   electric guitars.

■ ■ ■

Put aside your moral raiment and I
alone among them come forth to offer
a litany of ardor: my bride, my guide, my lady,
my baby, couch of wisdom, crystal meth
connection, green plastic garden pail,
ice-covered pencil sharpener,
brand-new house in white-hot flames,
bright-painted gate to beautiful things,
interlocking dancer's thighs of black diamonds,
mystical video disk unfolding precisely
like flowers, tree-lined La Cienega to Hollywood
in Autumn, angel of the air, arriving
in clean reception, woman made of cities,
intricately busy with her own construction.

Once we were the issue of chaos, Marie, asleep
in the snows of virtue; now we wake up to
     mutual delight,
as priests and presidents wither into
     indefinite night.

Emergency

It's still dark, my chest is hollow, and aches,
salt tears drop onto my overcooked oatmeal,
then I must go out and meet the masses—
whole shoals of ruined spirits that flop
around my path like grunion, or echo dumb
replies like Chatty Cathies. I want to shout
through the cut-out slot I breathe through,
but I'm drowned out by the shrieking of these corpses
from their burning tombs: hell's great heresiarchs
compelling us to shrink from our desires.

Yet sometimes, in line for my lunchtime burrito,
I catch sight of two eyes, a nose, the lips
of a pretty saint, who points salaciously toward heaven.
Then I think of you, believe again in miracles.
Maybe I can get you on the phone tonight.

And by the time I'm making dinner, I'm not
so much another big dummy, as a Lazarus
ready to rejoin the living: I have killed
my puppet, that grim traitor, and I autonomously
walk and talk. So I put on a record
and actually dance as the Whispers are moaning, "Operator,
Got to talk to her, This is an emergency!"
But when I finally call, no one answers.
Over there it's three hours later.
Where could you be? A big emptiness
begins to gulp me up, and the drift
of burning fish follows from the kitchen.

Heartbeat

Let me show you everything in the sky.
The sky is a concrete dome
all crusted over with jewels.
With the clear logic of a dream the dome
opens up—and there I hang.
Only the force-field of reality
holds me between the power of this exterior,
which forgoes the ornaments of romance,
and that interior, which commands me
to go for it. I let go, flopping in my affection,
and plop before you; and you suddenly smile.
Or else you sit in my passenger seat
and sing along with "Heartbeat". Now every
gadget in the city jams up and
I make my confession: "Oh, baby,
I really really like you. Pay back
the money I lent you and let's go
to the Planetarium." In the dark
I make my move and your soft pulse is
at my fingertips as we both pretend
to look toward heaven. But there I see
my reverence has crystalized you
into a Diana, and your and everybody's
eyes are red inlaid gems, indistinguishable
as the constellations on spring nights
when you're drunk and you can't find Mars.
I'm drunk and I can't find you.

You Make Everything Move Me

Kissing out on the patio.
I drove all night to get here: swish, my pretty breakfast.
You say, hey, I didn't give you any false ideas.
I say I didn't recognize you when I felt this new love.
You are shorter, your hair falls forward.
To the pool then, racing arm in arm.
I sing "Wild Thing" out loud—it never sounded better.

Tiny Histories

This is what we have:
we have endurance,

we have the eloquent example
of numbers: the dinosaurs lived

one-hundred-and-fifty million years, my love,
and we have our tiny histories,

which seem real enough: the daily
frictions in general, your

incessant typing in particular.
These small things bring us close

to a story even we know the end of.
Sometimes we sit, waiting to be sad,

because it is always difficult,
even when it is easy. I know.

I had to spoof one or two demons
just to get here, to this familiar bed,

to you: we have, at times
this momentum only, this current

which pulls us toward one another, flush
with oblivion.

Desperate Message #1 (History)

When the jets crowd close to the house tops,
and the thunder of their passing shakes
the droplets from the leaves of the chestnut tree,
and they fall in dull groups, punctuating the dust,
and when there is time to consider the cool, grey sky,
to wake to its many hues and its sway,
its hovering, fluorescent mood that seems right,
in the way the past is right, or unalterable—
then see how the days are full of false modesty,
how they fall neatly one on top the other,
the shadow coming full circle around the tree,
and see how they vanish and then add up to you,
in a chair, in an empty room, in a house . . .

Desperate Message #2

Not the end of the world,
but a mouthful of salt water
sends you shuttling against the slope,
against the difficult pull of the surf.
Not the buried wish, rocketed forth, at last,
but seven sleek mackerel,
together in a flash before your eyes,
leap from their pursuer.
No private end, no melodrama
by cartridge or clip, the fine smell of bluing,
the slip of the knot that stops the neck—
none of that. Against the coast line, that roar
is the ocean's steady method,
hammering the pinnacles with a vengeance
that knows nothing is ever finished,
neither erosion, nor hope
nor the endless harvest of speech.

Desperate Message #3 (Desire)

Their hands have found in each other
the impossibility of bodies.
They gather what they can.
Here, and here, in the tangled turn,
in the soft, suede taper of the neck,
in desire, they are wise
to the body's overflowing reticence:
nothing is ever enough is the joke
that keeps giving itself to us,
the air calm, the trees lime-colored,
the hands, like tourists without visas,
cameras without film, busily, purposefully,
taking picture after picture after picture.

COLE SWENSEN

Through Eyes

like the leopard's
all black
through distance
in the distance
antelope
look like the flames
one will soon become
in his veins.
And if a calm machinery
sharpens, shoulders
firing themselves like shot
and the one thing
this leopard's never figured out:
How this deer
floats up to him,
how his own reflection disappears
out the back of its eye.

Distant Children

Those little girls sound
like birds she said running
through the dusk in the courtyard
of the hotel deepening slightly
startled she
likes it that way. The edge
of confusion seeming
soft for an edge, the
girls too seemingly
losing definition.
The two men agreed.
They were strangers and seemed kind.
"yes, like bright red birds"
it grew darker.
Now we find our way
by the smell of the orange trees.

Three Hours

I have a small but present eternity here with me today, three hours, which remind me of nights when I was a child. I had the not-altogether-exaggerated notion that if you did not fall asleep, night would never end. In the first of these three hours, night has begun to fall in little chips that coat first the corners, the undersides and then the streets. Of course, I also had the notion that the heart was the only organ that a man could not live without, it being a piece of God, so you see, I may not be altogether trustworthy. But of these three hours, I have no doubt. Eternity can be a small thing and it can be closely observed. I will spend it, of course, reading. I will order coffees until I have to order them with equal parts milk, and I will watch night pile up in the streets like snow with the lights off. And I will read about Africa. And I will think it proves that eternity has a physical form, perhaps many of them, and I will look into the palm of my hand and become confused so I will raise my eyes and watch the hills closing in on themselves and be no less confused and I will, all this time, be reading. Which is like a television with no light on inside. Or talking to a very old aunt in a room growing dimmer, her cigarette glows. The explorers I am reading about were searching for the end of her cigarette, the end that enters the warmth of a mouth and the rivers that must sprout from there. So little was known of geography then. They thought that Africa was one with Antartica and they refuse to change their minds. They know nothing of how eternity changes. They argue about the direction of a certain river and yet insist that darkness flows only one way. That is because they are here, in this eternity, where the darkness is up to the knees and this book is their window and they can see perfectly well, those rivers of red light in the setting sun, running back into the heart of Africa from which God refuses to budge. We are lucky, we were born that way, so I order another cup of coffee and they drink it because they are determined not to fall asleep and I have seen nothing so far that has changed my mind.

Sheet

The difficult sleep of open windows
and the caravan
all but glimpsed; the sense
of someone following
In the heat which makes the world
an ancient thing
and the caravan
white in the whiter sun
and the addition, constant
or dropping of things
one by one. Whiter
In the sleep which makes
the heat an intimate thing
In the night in which we live
stark naked with the lights off
In the caravan a man is praying
while thinking about his birthplace
In the shadows your body is
sometimes erased
and I like that.

DAVID TRINIDAD

Meet the Supremes

When Petula Clark sang "Downtown," I wished I
could go there with her. I wanted to be free
to have fun and fall in love, but from suburbia
the city appeared more distant and dangerous
than it actually was. I withdrew and stayed
in my room, listened to Jackie DeShannon sing
"What The World Needs Now Is Love." I agreed,
but being somewhat morose considered the song
a hopeless plea. I listened to Skeeter Davis'
"The End Of The World" and decided that was
what it would be when I broke up with my first
boyfriend. My head spun as fast as the singles
I saved pennies to buy: "It's My Party," "Give
Him A Great Big Kiss," "(I Want To Be) Bobby's
Girl," "My Guy"—the list goes on. At the age
of ten, I rushed to the record store to get
"Little" Peggy March's smash hit, "I Will Follow
Him." An extreme example of lovesick devotion,
it held down the top spot on the charts for
several weeks in the spring of 1963. "Chapel
Of Love" came out the following year and was
my favorite song for a long time. The girls
who recorded it, The Dixie Cups, originally
called themselves Little Miss & The Muffets.
They cut three hits in quick succession, then
disappeared. I remember almost the exact moment
I heard "Johnny Angel" for the first time: it
came on the car radio while we were driving
down to Laguna Beach to visit some friends of
the family. In the back seat, I set the book I'd
been reading beside me and listened, completely
mesmerized by Shelley Fabares' dreamy, teenage
desire. Her sentimental lyrics continue to move
me (although not as intensely) to this day.

Throughout adolescence, no other song affected
    me quite like that one.
On my transistor, I listened to the Top Twenty
countdown as, week after week, more girl singers
    and groups
came and went than I could keep track of:

    Darlene Love,
    Brenda Lee,
    Dee Dee Sharp,
    Martha Reeves
    & The Vandellas,
    The Chantels,
    The Shirelles,
    The Marvelettes,
    The Ronettes,
    The Girlfriends,
    The Rag Dolls,
    The Cinderellas,
    Alice Wonderland,
    Annette, The
    Beach-Nuts, Nancy
    Sinatra, Little
    Eva, Veronica,
    The Pandoras,
    Bonnie & The
    Treasures,
    The Murmaids,
    Evie Sands,
    The Pussycats,
    The Patty Cakes,
    The Tran-Sisters,
    The Pixies Three,
    The Toys, The
    Juliettes and
    The Pirouettes,
    The Charmettes,
    The Powder Puffs,

Patti Lace &
The Petticoats,
The Rev-Lons,
The Ribbons,
The Fashions,
The Petites,
The Pin-Ups,
Cupcakes,
Chic-Lets,
Jelly Beans,
Cookies, Goodies,
Sherrys, Crystals,
Butterflys,
Bouquets,
Blue-Belles,
Honey Bees,
Dusty Springfield,
The Raindrops,
The Blossoms,
The Petals,
The Angels,
The Halos,
The Hearts,
The Flamettes,
The Goodnight
Kisses, The
Strangeloves,
and The Bitter
Sweets.

I was ecstatic when "He's So Fine" hit the #1 spot.
I couldn't get the lyrics out of my mind and continued
to hum "Doo-lang Doo-lang Doo-lang" long after
puberty ended, a kind of secret anthem. Although
The Chiffons tried to repeat their early success
with numerous singles, none did as well as their
first release. "Sweet Talkin' Guy" came close,
sweeping them back into the Top Ten for a short

time, but after that there were no more hits.
Lulu made her mark in the mid-sixties with "To Sir With Love,"
which I would put on in order to daydream about
my junior high algebra instructor. By then I was
a genuine introvert. I'd come home from school,
having been made fun of for carrying my textbooks
like a girl, and listen to song after song from
my ever-expanding record collection. In those
days, no one sounded sadder than The Shangri-Las.
Two pairs of sisters from Queens, they became famous
for their classic "death disc shocker," "Leader Of The Pack,"
and for their mod look. They were imitated (but never equalled)
by such groups as The Nu-Luvs and The Whyte Boots.
The Shangri-Las stayed on top for a couple of
years, then lost their foothold and split up.
Much later, they appeared in rock 'n' roll revival
shows, an even sadder act since Marge, the fourth
member of the band, had died of an accidental
drug overdose. I started smoking cigarettes around
this time, but wouldn't discover pills, marijuana
or alcohol until my final year of high school.
I loved Lesley Gore because she was always crying
and listened to "As Tears Go By" till the single had
so many scratches I couldn't play it anymore.
I preferred Marianne Faithful to The Beatles and
The Rolling Stones, was fascinated by the stories
about her heroin addiction and suicide attempt.
She's still around. So is Diana Ross. She made
it to superstardom alone, maintaining the success
she'd previously achieved as the lead singer of
The Supremes, one of the most popular girl groups
of all time. Their debut album was the first LP
I owned. Most of the songs on it were hits—
one would reach the top of the charts as another
hit the bottom. Little did I know, as I listened
to "Nothing But Heartaches" and "Where Did Our Love
Go," that nearly twenty years later I would hit
bottom in an unfurnished Hollywood single, drunk
and stoned and fed up, still spinning those same

and stoned and fed up, still spinning those same
old tunes. The friction that already existed
within The Supremes escalated in 1967 as Diana
Ross made plans for her solo career. The impending
split hit Florence the hardest. Rebelliously,
she gained weight and missed several performances,
and was finally told to leave the group. The pain
she experienced in the years that followed was
a far cry from the kind of anguish expressed
in The Supremes' greatest hits. Florence lost
the lawsuit she filed against Motown, failed at
a solo career of her own, went through a bitter
divorce, and ended up on welfare. In this classic
photograph of the group, however, Florence is
smiling. Against a black backdrop, she and Mary
look up at and frame Diana, who stands in profile
and raises her right hand, as if toward the future.
The girls' sequinned and tasselled gowns sparkle
as they strike dramatic poses among some Grecian
columns. Thus, The Supremes are captured forever
like this, in an unreal, silvery light. That
moment, they're in heaven. Then, at least for Flo,
begins the long and painful process of letting go.

Movin' with Nancy

It is almost time to grow up
I eat my TV dinner and watch
Nancy Sinatra in 1966
All boots and thick blonde hair

I eat my TV dinner and watch
The daughter of Frank Sinatra
All boots and thick blonde hair
She appears on "The Ed Sullivan Show"

The daughter of Frank Sinatra
She sings "These Boots Are Made For Walkin' "
She appears on "The Ed Sullivan Show"
The song becomes a number one hit

She sings "These Boots Are Made For Walkin' "
She sings "Somethin' Stupid" with her father
The song becomes a number one hit
She marries and divorces singer/actor Tommy Sands

She sings "Somethin' Stupid" with her father
She sings "The Last Of The Secret Agents"
She marries and divorces singer/actor Tommy Sands
She sings "How Does That Grab You, Darlin'?"

She sings "The Last Of The Secret Agents"
She sings "Lightning's Girl" and "Friday's Child"
She sings "How Does That Grab You, Darlin'?"
She sings "Love Eyes" and "Sugar Town"

■ ■ ■

She sings "Lightning's Girl" and "Friday's Child"
She puts herself in the hands of writer/producer Lee Hazelwood
She sings "Love Eyes" and "Sugar Town"
She co-stars with Elvis Presley in *Speedway*

She puts herself in the hands of writer/producer Lee Hazelwood
Three gold records later
She co-stars with Elvis Presley in *Speedway*
She rides on Peter Fonda's motorcycle

Three gold records later
She has developed an identity of her own
She rides on Peter Fonda's motorcycle
The wild angels roar into town

She has developed an identity of her own
Nancy Sinatra in 1966
The wild angels roar into town
It is almost time to grow up

JAMES ULMER

Crabbing for Blue-claws

We row along the shore on the bay side
to a spot my father knows.
He drives the steel hooks
through frozen bait, drops the oily 'bunkers
six feet to the bottom.

Along the inlet, cattails
and sea oats, the shoebox bungalows
in yellow and blue, everything familiar
on the coast where I was a boy.
Twenty years. A line jerks,

and he draws it in slowly,
The fish's white flesh in green water.
I scoop it up, netting a blue-claw
big enough to keep:
four inches from point to point,
the length of a beer can.

We're lucky. By noon,
we have fifteen keepers whispering and clicking
in a wicker basket.
When I look in, they raise their claws—
inky blue on the undersides, bands
of scarlet along the top pincers—

and scramble to the corners,
mouths open, their eyes on stems.

■ ■ ■

At home, my father
fills the Dutch oven
with beer, bay leaf, laurel and dill,
and when it starts to steam
he drops the crabs in.

They only struggle a moment;
then drift in the rolling boil.

Bright red, our catch
smokes on the table, cooling.

Each crab is a can to be opened.
He lifts the top shells
for the buttery lumps of backfin,
splits the claws with a nutcracker, and digs
in every joint for more of the snowy meat.
Later, he can't wash the smell
from his hands,

and each card he touches—
queen of clubs, jack of diamonds—
gives off a faint scent of carrion.

I can't keep my eyes open.
When I lie down, still feeling the water's motion,

I drift in the green current,
the shadow of my father's boat
a knife point above me, the sun
a new penny vanishing over my head.

From a Box of Old Photographs

The girl in the picture is seventeen.
Combs over each temple hold her dark hair back.
She leans into the arms of the tall sailor
behind her, who smiles at the camera.
She gazes at him over her shoulder, her lips

open slightly. Her grass skirt parts
and a sleek leg, bent at the knee,
points toward the camera. Her mouth and nails
look almost black. Chains of wildflowers
circle her ankles, wrists, and throat,

though it's not Hawaii but the Jersey marshland.
Hanging over the sea oats behind them,
a blue heron unfolds its wings, caught
mid-way in its lift to flight.
The man holding the picture is surprised

to find his mother so languid and beautiful.
He thinks of Lady crooning *Lover Man.*
The tall sailor is not his father,
and he recalls an old letter he found once
in an unfamiliar hand, about sleeping

under the water line, alone and not alone, bodies
huddled in the half-dark. If the ship
was still, you could hear a shark's tail slap
against the hull. The letter remembered her eyes,
gray like the ocean, bluer on sunny days.

These Nights

the full moon drains me.
White roses below my window

seem about to rise from their stems,
confused by so much light.

The shadows of streetlamps
describe a ladder I keep trying

to climb, hoping for ease, but gravity
holds me now. I walk our rooms:

leaded windows, brass doorknobs, ornaments
of coming and going. You wanted

to live here surrounded by roses, hornets
droning, the blossoms lasting

into winter—all this ruined now
by your absence. The time

you read my cards the five of cups
turned up—three cups spilled, two full—

and you warned me not to mourn.
Now the rooms swirl with a faint

■ ■ ■

dust, or pollen, in which my steps
leave no trace. I remember how

your breasts lifted and fell as you slept,
my uncertain ground, partly in shadow,

partly in light—How the moon
weaves through these blinds! Often

you would murmur in your sleep,
and I would lean close to listen.

Daily Bread

Ergot schlerotia has been identified
in a sample of wheat grown in western
Washington.
　　　　　　　—The Seattle Times

You sit in the yard and find
no reason to move. Everything
you need is here. Your eyes and ears
are open fully, enough to see
the rainbow in sunlight on brick.
The sycamore you lean against
is breathing—you hear it drawing
water up its long chain of xylem.
And the sky, the sky is not blue
but forty blues, and toward dusk
a pale green through which bats
trace their elaborate letters.
And later, when you return
to milking cows, mending
the split-rail fence, the substantiality
of stable and field, your daily bread,
you will know where you walk
is holy. Something rises from what you plant—
it is in the wheat,
those thousand thin women with their hair
on fire. Listen in the field—
what you hear is not the wind only.

The Uccello

1.

Into the chambers and antechambers
and dressing rooms of the dead enters
Leonardo in his malodorous contraptions.
To the tired tailor, tasting his familiar
mouthful of pins as he adjusts the shreds
of cloth swelling the air
(the motions of air being
as intricate as those of water),
even Lucifer's wardrobe was easier to sew,
though hot to his fingers.
Because Leonardo believed in the bat,
in the black jelly and web of its wing,
he has brought cane skeletons, leather tendons,
steel springs, and the membranes of starched
taffeta to procure his wings from the tailor.

In his infernal gymnasium
(the curtains hung as in an inferior
hotel and the anonymous sweat of others
left like cooking grease upon the walls), here,
Leonardo stoops, bends and unbends,
with his head pumps a piston and with his arms
turns the windlasses, causing four flippers
to oscillate and the tawdry curtains to lift
and part in the man-made wind.
(The nature of wind being
composed of its aqueous vowels.)

Where else may a man by night build himself
a rudder of sized linen, cane, and wire
to study the angle of a bird's wing's

response to vortices of air and by day
search the Corte Vecchia palace
for a suitable place to launch his flight?
Yes, this is Hell, though beautiful
to the tailor, who never had much call
in his own village. Even the colors of Hell
are more poignant to him than the remembered
sunset over the dirty river he left behind.
And how can he tell his wife in letter
how complex the diabolical pathways here,
carved by hand with the precision of a dozen
spheres laid each inside the other
from a single wooden block?
The father must teach the son such secret
linkage. It is the same way with the invisible
stitches he puts into a silk lining.

2.

So that we may escape the peril
of destruction, so that we find a means
to survive a tempest or shipwreck at sea,
we are blessed with the girdle of mind.
So we may abide our time drifting
in amnionic fluid, each fetus is given
its air-tube and three-chambered heart.
The human embryo must spend its prenatal
life in the chambers and antechambers
and dressing rooms of the dead,
doing its best through its leg motion,
arms, or on occasion both combined, to power
its small flying machine of cartilage and moss-
scented blood. As if the dream of flying
is the remembered navigation of the uterus
(thus the mirific synchroneity
between atmosphere and ocean),
the unborn memorize the physics of bouyancy
through the peck and suck of the womb's
bright berry. Doesn't the placenta's gel
tell of smashed holly, pokeweed, smilax, prickly pear?

The Black Bird's Golden House

I remember my mother in the doorway,
a great black bird.
But I would not name it, name her, would
not say the words: *raven, mockingbird, crow.*
I could only call her the black bird,
not *rook, magpie, jay, jackdaw.*
Under the white feather of her dress, her
   hands
were two bitter fruits, calling me in.
She ate her own hands around the horns
of nail, white bone sucked soft.
I knew the mockingbird ate wild berries.
Gnawed her hands ragged and clean, dry.
The black bird. The black bird.
I followed her in.
I placed in my mouth, gently, each bitter
finger of fruit: tasting mulberry, grape, juniper.
I followed her in. I did.

I followed a magpie home.
Do not bring the magpie back, my mother
warned, it is a bad sign.
Into the thorny bush went the magpie and I.
Am I an angel
or only a bird,
with these two dark omens,
these black wings, tacked on my back?
I could not be sure who spoke.
It might have been the magpie.
It could very well have been myself.

■ ■ ■

My mother did not sing.
Could not, would not.
Tone-deaf as the beggar woman
calling for her coins.
I hear my mother singing now
with the crows, I think.
Singing harsher than tin
plates that clink on air
(we strung them together
to chase birds from her garden).
Crows are clever, they don't scare.
They sing with her.
My own voice rises:
throaty as crows talking.
I can't sing, either.
We sing, we sing!
Oh mocker, oh mother.

Why do they bury small birds
in cigar boxes? Some birds learn
to love the smell of Dutch Masters
the way they love death.
My father has many thin tins of Willem II.
They come from Holland, a long way.
No bird would ever fit inside.
My mother uses them for holding
rubber bands inside a drawer.
I think the sound of a bird's bill
upon the tin would be pretty.
There is a sheet of waxy paper inside,
folded once. It smells of cigars
on that paper long after the tin is empty.
A crow's wings smell of wind
long after it dies. This is the way
smell is: it lingers.
Fold yourself into the box, sleep,
I heard the crow say it.

■ ■ ■

This is the eye that mocks my father,
this is the eye that disobeys my mother:
the ravens of the valley shall pick it out.
My mother was dying.
I brought my eye for her, the eye
the ravens took. I fed her bread
and flesh. She was Elijah.
I was a raven. I brought her the eye.
She would not die.
I took it away again.
I had to.
I built her a house
under the table, all gold, like Solomon's.
I was not wise, I wasn't a king,
but I could build her a golden place
under the table. Even the table legs
were gold, shining.
It would take me years.
I would carve the cherubim of olive-wood,
as he did. I would make the gold vessels.
The birds, flying, said: candlestick, lamp,
tong, cup, basin, basin. They said basin
twice. I don't know why. Hinges,
they said. I did not wonder. I built.
I opened my mother's box
of earrings and pendants: I saw
the Earth revolve as her box of precious:
each bird thinking, *I am light, I am fire.*
Amethyst, ruby. Ruby, a fire of ruby.
Sapphire and granite. Topaz. Lapis lazuli.
The earth revolved. I fell. I built
my house of gold. She could not die
in a gold house. She did not.
And her hair inside the house,
I combed her hair. It was black
and healthy as Solomon's, raven hair.
Glossy, almost purple.
My own stayed light but had shadows
like birds whose shadows seem to fly
through glass while their bodies remain outside.

CYNTHIA ZARIN

The Near and Dear

I   WHERE YOU ARE
Paris, and all the streets muffled,
the copper glare of windows, the click-click
over the drain grate. I can't be where
you are, the melodeon incessant
in the background, two students
sprawled like cats across the bar.
                    But in New York,
you are saying, and even your old clothes
seem to shine, mother-of-pearl
in the low-light, and I am kissing you,
kissing you good-bye.

II   ELSEWHERE
We take up residence, elsewhere.
Elsewhere, a packet boat
slow on the Potomac, shade
trees, mosquitoes bridling
in the scuppernong.
What was once a different country
resettles in the arbor—lamplight
pooling on the room's
plaited tail ends, times of day,
daylight clumping in the thorny hedges.

What was once, then, is:
column after column, the homestead
reflects in its own pond, where
house after house surfaces, then
drifts (one burned, one altered
by the sleeping porch, the shed)—
the family fortune, out rowing
in little boats.

■ ■ ■

The pond is full, tight net of
water lilies in the blade-thin hush.

Time gone, then, in the blade-thin hush.
In this little country of the soul,
another country curls into itself,
the house with its cornices, its
crenellations. And thought takes wing
to clear a wider space—landing,
falling in the garden.

III   THE PIGEONS

Stone lion by the gatehouse, and
all the pigeons, preening themselves.
Homing pigeons, you said, or doves,
the morning they blew to the window,
high over the duck pond, over the rosebushes.
Cooing in the ivy, and all the horrible ruckus—
I hated their dark wallow in the rafters.
Squawking barnacles, vertiginous—at noon
the black-clad friars fed their belching crowd,
acres of bread, gobble over the piazza.

IV   FABLE

A day catching blue marlin
in the warm bay—he told me about her
kiss, the shape of it, how he
could hear the sea in it.

Clams for supper,
a rotting set of Balzac
on the sleeping porch, girls and soldiers
in old *Life* magazines, their glassy
gray patina. Four thunderstorms
off the Chesapeake, smoke billowing
from a gigantic train—the house
was a cavern of dark and whitewashed rafters,
his sister's doll house took up
half the room.

V   *COR CORDIUM*

Keats' house, and all the paraphernalia
of journeys, midnight returns—two locks
of hair, fastened in a blue glass. It's all
so secretive, the narrow stair to the shrine,
the four versions of his body,
burning near the pine grove. You can go
to the pine grove, think of it,
the family jokes, the masquerades,
the sweetheart dogs and children
tight bundled in the carriage.

Think of it, the ride back—the scene
whizzes by, and you stare down at Florence,
flung like a brocade across the valley.
Imagine, then, the road to the villa
ending, and they open the door and you
break the news.

VI   THE NEAR AND DEAR

Daily. Daily, the clouds lagging
over the marsh come faster, the sky
pushing behind them, and three days running
a compass point of birds, a chevron
marking time of day, then time of year.

Daylight, and far over the harbor
the vista with its flapping sails,
milk cans cluttering up the prow.
But wait, a house full of bells and calls,
a house with room after room
of trees: table, chairs, the bedpost carved
to look like a sapling. Ring after ring,
the bell is calling you to dinner
—to shape your napkin into a bird—
and I am calling you, calling out your name,
love like an aubade of bells,
a solitary ringing from the steeple.

Pears Soap

Transparence a virtue, as in prose or water,
though not lies; like good news from a far country,
the Pears soap's rider of ingredients—thyme, cedar,
glycerine—comes affiched with a baroque postage
stamp, a filigre signet, familiar as a cigar band:
by appointment to Her Majesty the Queen, since

seventeen-eighty-nine; the year (one looks it up)
Eclipse, the famous racehorse, died; Blake published *Songs
of Innocence*, and, boarded with its Latin cousins,
fuschia and hortensia, the chrysanthemum
was introduced from the Orient, into England.
Also the year King George, mad, retrieved his senses.

Through the yellow bathroom's frosted glass, the urban
morning is a dun frieze, a grisaille, and the gold
soap a chrysalis; a stained glass lozenge, a pane
from the neverending Thragelia: harvest
of soot, getting over it, sorrow a fly
in amber—Chryseis, back in Rome, after Apollo's

pestilence; Blake's boy in his chrome chrysanthemum,
glad after experience, and the soap, slipped from
my wrinkling hand, a bronze-winged partridge, squatting on
the porcelain—partridge a Midlands alias
of Roman umber—its name washing off but its
clear self still left, reversal of the usual death.

The Swordfish Tooth

An Erté obelisk, a spire, the solitary
letter *I*, a stopped metronome, cool, wooden,
infinitely beleaguered, bland as an unlit
cigarette. Upright, the swordfish tooth,
a sickbed gift, plays didactic marionette.
Sickness is punishment, says Fever;
like Pinocchio, one's made oneself grotesque
for telling random, half-forgotten lies.
This flu's genesis is Asian—like innocence
of war at home, it fells Americans under forty.

Reviewing the previous week's events,
Christmas is the culprit. Us, childless,
set on by the family's provender
of battery-powered phlegmish angels: maraschino
lights switched on, their sweatshirts
spelled out, infectiously, *Joyeux Noel*.
Two days later found us entombed, punch
drunk on brandy, rose hips, and microbes.
Decades and distance make us orphans,
childhood a loose tooth, tied to a thread.

Simple prayer: If I fall, let it be
on this cottage-cum-house's hand knotted
turtle and flower Turkish rug. Thus.
After a week of Penguin's recycled
picaresques (pink-cheeked barristers
advising lower-case saints in Dorset)
accompanied by influenza's rites—
chills, headache, complaints, the telephone
unplugged—recovery. Beer all around
to celebrate. The tooth, clinging to grit,

■ ■ ■

forlorn, unattached, long as my arm,
washed up by the syzgic tide; Earth, Sun,
and Moon, in what the meteorologists
persist in calling "an unusual line,"
is, if nothing else, a paddle.
And I, a bleary seal in my nightgown,
roused, repentent, still bewitched,
loath to be called an ungrateful child;
the swordfish tooth, non sequitur, a certainty
to cleave the soul back to the spine.

ABOUT THE POETS

Judith Baumel is assistant professor of English at Adelphi University. Her book *The Weight of Numbers* won the 1987 Walt Whitman Award of the Academy of American Poets and was published by Wesleyan in 1988. A graduate of Radcliffe College and the Johns Hopkins writing seminars, Judith Baumel received a New York Foundation for the Arts grant and has served as director of the Poetry Society of America.

Bruce Beasley is the author of *Spirituals* (Wesleyan University Press, 1988). A native of Macon, Georgia, he graduated from Oberlin College and received an MFA at Columbia University. He lives in Charlottesville, Virginia.

April Bernard's first book of poems, *Blackbird Bye Bye*, won the 1988 Walt Whitman Prize from the Academy of American Poets and is being published by Random House in the spring of 1989. She is at work on a novel and a play and has written the screenplay adaptation of the Jane Bowles novel *Two Serious Ladies*.

Lucie Brock-Broido received her MA from Johns Hopkins University and her MFA from Columbia University. She has held poetry fellowships from the National Endowment for the Arts, the Fine Arts Work Center in Provincetown, the Artists Foundation, and the Hoyns Fellowship. She lives in Boston and is Briggs-Copeland Lecturer in Poetry at Harvard University.

Cyrus Cassells was born in Delaware in 1957 and was raised primarily in California. He received his BA from Stanford University, where he was awarded the Academy of American Poets Prize. He is the author of *The Mud Actor* (Holt, 1982), a National Poetry Series selection. He has been a recipient of fellowships from the National Endowment for the Arts, the Massachusetts Artists Foundation, and the Fine Arts Work Center in Provincetown. He is an actor as well as a writer and has traveled extensively throughout the United States and abroad.

Henri Cole was born in 1956 in Fukuoka, Japan. He grew up in Virginia and was graduated from the College of William and Mary. He holds graduate degrees from the University of Wisconsin and Columbia University and is the recipient of fellowships from the Ingram Merrill Foundation and the New York Foundation for the Arts. His poems have been published in *Antaeus, Grand Street, The Nation, The Paris Review,* and *Poetry,* and his first full-length collection, *The Marble Queen,* was published in 1986 by Atheneum. He lives in New York City.

Connie Deanovich has been published in *New American Writing, Shiny International, Oovrah, Another Chicago Magazine,* and elsewhere. Born on November 8, 1960, she works as an editorial freelancer and is a master's candidate in English and American literature at DePaul University, Chicago.

Lynn Doyle currently teaches at the University of Houston. Her book of poems *Living Gloves* (Dutton, 1986) was selected by Cynthia Macdonald in the 1985 National Poetry Series open competition. *Poetry Northwest* awarded her its Young Poet's Prize in 1984 and the *Pushcart Prize, 1984–85* listed her as an "Outstanding Writer of Poetry." She received graduate degrees in English from both the University of Houston and the University of Virginia.

Cornelius Eady was born and raised in Rochester, New York. His books of poetry are *Kartunes* (1980), *Victims of the Latest Dance Craze* (1986), and a chapbook, *Boom Boom Boom* (1988). His awards include an NEA grant, a fellowship in poetry at the Breadloaf Writer's Conference, and the 1985 Lamont Prize from the Academy of American Poets. At present, he lives and teaches in New York.

Martin Edmunds was born in Waltham, Massachusetts, in 1955. He received his BA from Harvard College and went through Boston University's MA program in creative writing. He is a writer-in-residence at the Cathedral of St. John the Divine in Manhattan, where he lives with his wife, Carol Moldaw.

Elaine Equi was born and grew up in Oak Park, Illinois. Her books include *Federal Woman, Shrewcrazy, The Corners of the Mouth,* and, most recently, *Accessories.* She has given many readings throughout the country and currently lives in New York.

Martín Espada is the author of *The Immigrant Iceboy's Bolero* (Waterfront Press) and *Trumpets from the Islands of Their Eviction* (Bilingual Press, Arizona State University). He has been awarded a Massachusetts Artists Fellowship (1984), a

National Endowment for the Arts Fellowship (1986), a Boston Contemporary Writers Award (1987), and the Rosalie Boyle Award (1987). He currently lives in Boston, where he works as a tenant lawyer.

Kathy Fagan's first book, *The Raft*, a winner of the 1985 National Poetry Series open competition, was published by E. P. Dutton in May 1985. She has been a recipient of an Ingram Merrill Foundation grant and is currently teaching at Cal Poly in San Luis Obispo, California.

Suzanne Gardinier was born in New Bedford and grew up in Scituate, Massachusetts. She graduated from the University of Massachusetts at Amherst in 1981 and from the Columbia MFA program in 1986. Having worked as a Pinkerton's security guard, night-shift doughnut baker, student organizer, Woolworth's Christmas cashier, Haight-Ashbury liquor store clerk, Cambridge bookstore clerk, and temporary secretary, she is now assistant editor of *Grand Street*.

Martha Hollander has contributed poems to various magazines, including *Shenandoah, Partisan Review*, and *Grand Street. Always History*, a chapbook of her work, appeared in 1985. She is presently working on a doctorate in the history of art at Berkeley.

Lynda Hull was born in New Jersey. *Ghost Money*, her first collection, was published by the University of Massachussetts Press as the 1986 winner of its Juniper Prize competition. Her poems have appeared in *The New Yorker, Poetry, Antioch Review*, and elsewhere. She holds degrees from the University of Arkansas and Johns Hopkins University. She is presently teaching in the MFA Writing Program of Vermont College and is poetry editor for the journal *Crazyhorse*.

Vickie Karp was born in New York City. She is on the staff of *The New Yorker* and is currently completing a first collection of poems. In 1988 her film on Marianne Moore aired on PBS and her play on the friendship of Moore and Elizabeth Bishop was staged at the Symphony Space Theater in New York.

Wayne Koestenbaum graduated from Harvard College in 1980, and subsequently earned a masters degree from the writing seminars of Johns Hopkins University and a Ph.D. from Princeton University. He is now an assistant professor of English at Yale University. His critical study on the erotics of male literary collaboration, *Double Talk*, was recently published by Routledge, and his poems have appeared in many journals, including *Ontario Review, The Antioch Review, Boulevard, The Quarterly*, and *Shenandoah*.

Victoria Kohn was born in New York City in 1958. She graduated from the Nightingale-Bamford School and Hamilton College. Her poems have appeared in *The Quarterly, Rolling Stone*, and *Maine Life*.

Robert McDowell's book of narrative poetry, *Quiet Money*, was published in 1987 by Henry Holt and Company, Inc. The publisher and chief editor of Story Line Press, McDowell also coedits *The Reaper*, a magazine devoted to the resurgence of narrative in contemporary poetry, with Mark Jarman. He lives in Santa Clara, California.

Askold Melnyczuk was raised in Cranford, New Jersey, and has worked as a dishwasher, a bartender, an editor, and an assistant bricklayer in a Ukrainian monastery in Italy. In 1972 he founded the literary journal *Agni*, which he resumed editing, after a seven-year leave, in 1987. His first published poem appeared in *The Village Voice* in 1974 and since then poems, stories, and translations from the Ukrainian, as well as reviews and essays, have come out in *Poetry, Witness, Partisan Review, Parnassus, The Missouri Review, Ploughshares*, and numerous other journals. He studied at Antioch College, the Newark College of Arts and Sciences (Rutgers), and Boston University (MA, 1978), where he now teaches.

Carol Moldaw was born in Oakland, California, in 1956 and raised in the San Francisco Bay Area. She received her BA from Harvard-Radcliffe College in 1979 and her MA in creative writing from Boston University in 1986. She lives in New York City with her husband, Martin Edmunds.

Karen Murai is a graduate of Columbia College, Chicago, Illinois, where she edited an award-winning anthology of student writing, *Hair Trigger 8 & 9*. Her work has appeared in *New American Writing* (previously *Oink!*), *B-City*, and student publications. One of her poems, "A Middle Class Monologue," won a 1987 Illinois Arts Council Literary Award.

230

Jane Oliensis studied Classics and English at Harvard and Columbia and has taught ancient Greek literature and language at several high schools and universities. She currently lives in Assisi, Italy, and has studied biblical Greek at the theological institute there.

Brenda Marie Osbey attended Dillard University, Universite Paul Valéry at Montpélliér, France, and the University of Kentucky at Lexington. A native of New Orleans, she presently teaches Afro-American literature at the University of California at Los Angeles. She has been a fellow of the MacDowell Colony, the Kentucky Foundation for Women, the Millay Colony, the Fine Arts Work Center at Provincetown, and the Bunting Institute of Radcliffe College, Harvard University. She is the author of *Ceremony for Minneconjoux* (Callaloo Poetry Series, 1983; University Press of Virginia 1985), *In These Houses* (Wesleyan University Press, 1988) and *2 Plus 2* (Mylabris Press, 1987).

Jacqueline Osherow's first book of poems, *Looking for Angels in New York*, was published by the University of Georgia Press in 1988. Her work has appeared in *The New Yorker*, the *Times Literary Supplement, Shenandoah*, and *Tikkun*, and is forthcoming in *The Georgia Review* and *The Denver Quarterly*, as well as *New York Gedichte*, an anthology of poems about New York to be published in Germany. She has studied at Harvard-Radcliffe, Trinity College, Cambridge (where she received the University Chancellor's Medal for an English Poem), and is now working on her Ph.D, in English literature at Princeton.

Donald Revell was born in New York City. His first collection, *From the Abandoned Cities*, was published in 1983 by Harper & Row. His second, *The Gaza of Winter*, was published in 1988 by the University of Georgia Press. He won a Pushcart Prize for poetry in 1985 and was a National Endowment for the Arts Fellow for 1988.

Mary Jo Salter was born in Grand Rapids, Michigan, and grew up in Baltimore. She has been the recipient of a National Endowment for the Arts fellowship and a cowinner of the "Discovery"/*The Nation* award. She is the author of two books of poems, *Henry Purcell in Japan* (Knopf, 1985) and *Unfinished Painting* (Knopf, 1989), which was the Lamont Poetry Selection for 1988 from the Academy of American Poets. She is also the author of a children's book, *The Moon Comes Too* (Knopf, 1989).

Vijay Seshadri was born in India, grew up in Ohio, and now lives in Brooklyn. He holds a BA from Oberlin College, an MFA from Columbia University, and is currently working toward a doctorate at the Department of Middle Eastern Languages and Cultures at Columbia. His poems and essays have appeared in numerous magazines and he has received a New York Foundation for the Arts Poetry fellowship.

Jason Shinder was born in Brooklyn, New York, in 1955. He is the author of the poetry chapbook *End of the Highest Balcony* (Purdue-Indiana University). His awards include a poetry fellowship from the Fine Arts Work Center in Provincetown and his work has appeared in *American Poetry Review* and elsewhere. He is also the editor of *Divided Light: Father & Son Poems* (Sheep Meadow Press) and general series interviewer for *The Essential Poets Cassettes: Poets on Essential Poets of the Past* (Ecco Press).

Jack Skelley is the author of a book of poems (*Monsters*, Little Caesar Press, 1982) and two novel fragments (*From Fear of Kathy Acker* and *More Fear of Kathy Acker*, Illuminati Press, 1985). During the early eighties he edited the pop-culture-centered *Barney: The Modern Stone-Age Magazine*. He has been a director at Beyond Baroque Literary/Arts Center in Venice, California. Skelley is also a rock musician who has recorded two albums with the all-instrumental group Lawndale for SST Records.

Mark Svenvold lives in Seattle, Washington, where he is studying English literature and Spanish at the University of Washington. His work has appeared in various magazines, including *Catalyst*, *MSS* (Manuscripts), and *Fine Madness*. His chapbook *Peripheries* appeared in 1982. He is completing a full-length manuscript, entitled *Desperate Messages*.

Cole Swensen was born in 1955 and currently lives in San Francisco. She received her MA in creative writing from San Francisco State University, where she subsequently taught as a lecturer. Her latest book, *New Math*, was selected for the National Poetry Series in 1987 and published by William Morrow and Company in 1988. Her first collection, *It's Alive She Says*, was published by Floating Island Press in 1984. She was awarded an Individual Artist's Grant from the Marin Arts Council in 1987.

David Trinidad was born and raised in Southern California. He received his BA in English from California State University at Northridge, where he studied poetry with Ann Stanford. His books include *Monday, Monday* (Cold Calm Press, 1985), *November* (Hanuman Books, 1987), and *Pavane* (Illuminati, 1988). He currently lives in Brooklyn, New York.

James Ulmer is a graduate of the University of Houston's creative writing program. His awards include two Academy of American Poets Prizes, a Hoyns Fellowship, the Pablo Neruda Prize from *Nimrod*, and the PEN Southwest Houston Discovery Award. Ulmer is writer-in-residence at Houston Baptist University.

Valerie Wohlfeld was born in California in 1956. She received her MFA in writing from Vermont College. Her work has appeared in *The New Yorker, Columbia, Nimrod, The North American Review, Epoch*, and *Quarterly West*. She is presently living in Newburyport, Massachusetts.

Cynthia Zarin was born in 1959 in New York City, grew up on Long Island, and was educated at Harvard and Columbia. Her poems have appeared in *The New Yorker, Grand Street, The Paris Review, The Yale Review*, and other magazines and her first collection, *The Swordfish Tooth*, was published by Knopf in 1989. She lives in New York City and is a staff writer for *The New Yorker*.

ACKNOWLEDGMENTS

Grateful acknowledgement is made to the following for permission to print their copyrighted material:

Judith Baumel: "The New York City World's Fairs, 1939 and 1964," "Proper Distance and Proper Time," and "Orcio and Fiasco" are reprinted by permission of Wesleyan University Press from *The Weight Of Numbers* by Judith Baumel. Copyright © 1988 by Judith Baumel. "Proper Distance and Proper Time" first appeared in *The Paris Review.* "Fish Speaking Veneto Dialect" is printed by permission of Judith Baumel. Copyright © 1988 by Judith Baumel.

Bruce Beasley: "Sleeping in Santo Spirito" is reprinted by permission of Bruce Beasley. Copyright © 1988 by Bruce Beasley. This poem first appeared in *The Quarterly.* "Childhood" and "The Reliquary" are reprinted by permission of Wesleyan University Press from *Spirituals* by Bruce Beasley. Copyright © 1988 by Bruce Beasley.

April Bernard: "The Way We Live Now" and "Elephant Languor" are reprinted by permission of Random House, Inc., from *Blackbird Bye Bye* by April Bernard. Copyright © 1989 by April Bernard.

Lucie Brock-Broido: "Ten Years Apprenticeship in Fantasy," "After the Grand Perhaps," and "Domestic Mysticism" are reprinted by permission of Alfred A. Knopf, Inc., from *A Hunger* by Lucie Brock-Broido. Copyright © 1988 by Lucie Brock-Broido.

Cyrus Cassells: "La Luna Verde," "Bound Feet," "The Pillow," and "Typhoon" are reprinted by permission of Henry Holt and Company, Inc., from *The Mud Actor* by Cyrus Cassells. Copyright © 1982 by Cyrus Cassells.

Henri Cole: "V-Winged and Hoary" and "Desert Days on the Reservoir" are reprinted by permission of Atheneum Publishers, an imprint of Macmillan Publishing Company, from *The Marble Queen* by Henri Cole. Copyright © 1986 by Henri Cole. "V-Winged and Hoary" originally appeared in *Antaeus.*

236